Everyday Adventures

EVERYDAY ADVENTURES

SAMUEL SCOVILLE Jr.

Republished by the
South Jersey Culture & History Center, 2018

This edition published 2018
by the South Jersey Culture & History Center

South Jersey Culture & History Center,
Stockton University,
101 Vera King Farris Drive
Galloway, New Jersey 08205

Title: Everyday Adventures
Author: Samuel Scoville Jr.

This book is dedicated to that brave and loyal adventurer, who has shared so many everyday adventures with me—my wife.

CONTENTS

FOREWORD

Samuel Scoville Jr. (1872–1950) was an attorney, writer, public speaker, ardent naturalist—and an adventurer, although of the quieter sort. Born in Norwich, New York, Scoville was the grandson of the famous nineteenth-century preacher Henry Ward Beecher. He attended Yale University, practiced law in Philadelphia for over fifty years, and adored reading, occupations which filled his "narrow in-door days," but when he could, he spent his time in nature, "his out-of-door days."

He joined the Delaware Valley Ornithological Club, one of the nation's oldest birding organizations, in 1907, and enjoyed taking part in frequent field trips with Witmer Stone, George Stuart III, J. Fletcher Street, and others.[1] Scoville took on the role of recorder and reporter for DVOC excursions, often reworking his notes and publishing them as essays in magazines such as *The Atlantic Monthly*, *Good Housekeeping*, *The Youth's Companion*, as columns in the Philadelphia *Evening Bulletin* (his nom de plume was "A Philadelphia Lawyer"), or as chapters in his books.

Everyday Adventures describes Scoville's jaunts into nature, introducing readers to hibernating mammals, snakes, orchids, and other flora, but most especially to birds. Scoville and his DVOC associates, whose identities are hidden by nicknames—"the botanist," "the banker," "the artist," and "the architect," partake in numerous explorations to locate and identify avian species. Each successful encounter is beautifully detailed and accompanied by phonetic birdcalls. Whether listening to the birdsong of unseen birds, searching for hidden nesting places, or quietly observing the daily routines of birds in nature, Scoville describes his surroundings vividly, often with considerable wit. Quickly, readers find that they have stepped into the story for an everyday adventure of their own.

With a naturalist's discerning eye, Scoville recounts expeditions in Connecticut, the Berkshires, Pennsylvania, Delaware, the Pine Barrens, and the far north of Canada. Some of his reports, such as when he describes a raven's nest high on a cliff in the Poconos, were considerable contributions to ornithology.[2] With equal detail and relish, he recounts day trips with his four children, aptly named the Band and, like his DVOC colleagues, provided with nicknames. Two years before the publication of *Everyday Adventures*, Scoville had described his children: "I have three [boys] of my own here and one that waits for me beyond, to say nothing of a little girl who is worth the world and all to us."[3] His obvious affection for his children, and the enjoyment he conveys when introducing nature to them, is one of the pleasures of this volume. It is not surprising that during his career Scoville organized and ran dozens of boys' clubs and was very active with the Boy Scouts. In fact, the five titles for young adults in his Boy Scout series were among his best-known works.

Although Scoville was not a collector in the typical ornithological sense—he did not collect eggs or nests or the birds themselves—he thought of his out-of-doors adventures as collecting, and preserved the best examples, like pressed flowers, for readers to return to and admire.

Angela Mazzara & Tom Kinsella, 2018

1   Julian K. Potter, "Samuel Scoville Jr.," *Cassinia* 38 (1951): 1–3.

2   Witmer Stone, Review: "Scoville's *Everyday Adventures*," *The Auk* 38, no. 1 (January 1921), 138–39.

3   *Twenty-Five Year Record, Class of Ninety-Three, Yale College* (New Haven, CT: The Tuttle, Morehouse & Taylor Company, 1918), 361–62.

For the sick and the sorry and the weary at heart stands a refuge at their very doors. There needs but sight to the unseeing eyes and the unstopping of deafened ears, and the way to the World where the sweet Wild Folk dwell lies open. Therein is happiness that time cannot tarnish, the stilling of sorrow and rest from toil. Let him who hears the call heed it as he values his soul's welfare.

I

EVERYDAY ADVENTURES

All that May day long I had been trying to break my record of birds seen and heard between dawn and dark. Toward the end of the gray afternoon an accommodating Canadian warbler, wearing a black necklace across his yellow breast, carried me past my last year's mark, and I started for home in great contentment. My path wound in and out among the bare white boles of a beech wood, all feathery with new green-sanguine-colored leaves. Always, as I enter that wood, I have a sense of a sudden silence, and I walk softly, that I may catch perhaps a last word or so of what they are saying.

That day, as I moved without a sound among the trees, suddenly, not fifty feet away, loping wearily down the opposite slope, came a gaunt red fox and a cub. With her head down, she looked like the picture of the wolf in Red Riding Hood. The little cub was all woolly, like a lamb. His back was reddish brown, and he had long stripes of gray across his breast and around his small belly, and his little sly face was so comical that I laughed at the very first sight of it. What wind there was blew from them to me, and my khaki clothes blended with the coloring around me.

As I watched them, another larger cub trotted down the hill. The first cub suddenly yapped at him, with a snarling little bark quite different from that of a dog; but the other paid no attention, but stalked sullenly into a burrow which for the first time I noticed among the roots of a white oak tree. Back of the burrow lay a large chestnut log, which evidently served as a watch-tower for the fox family. To this the mother fox went, and climbing up on top of it, lay down with her head on her paws and her magnificent brush dangling down beside the log, and went to sleep.

The little cub that was left trotted to the entrance of the burrow and for a while played by himself, like a puppy or a kitten. First, he snapped at some blades of grass and chewed them up fiercely. Then, seeing a leaf that had stuck in the wool on his back, he whirled around and around, snapping at it with his little jaws. Failing to catch it, he rolled over and over in the dirt until he had brushed it off. Then, he proceeded to stalk the battered carcass of an old black crow that lay in front of the burrow. Crouching and creeping up on it inch by inch, he suddenly sprang and caught that unsuspecting corpse and worried it ferociously, with fierce little snarls.

All the time his wrinkled-up, funny little face was so comical that I nearly laughed aloud every time he moved. At last he curled up in a round ball, with his chin on his forepaws like his mother.

There before me, at the end of the quiet spring afternoon, two of the wildest and shyest of all of our native animals lay asleep. Never before had I seen a fox in all that country, nor even suspected that one had a home within a scant mile of mine. As I watched them sleeping, I felt somehow that the wildwood had taken me into her confidence and was trusting her children to my care; and I would no more have harmed them, than I would my own.

As I watched the cub curled up in a woolly ball, I wanted to creep up and stroke his soft fur. Leaving the hard path, I started to cover as silently as possible the fifty feet that lay between us. Before I had gone far, a leaf rustled underfoot, and in a second the cub was on his feet, wide awake, and staring down at me. With one foot in the air, I waited and waited until he settled down to sleep again. A minute later the same thing happened once more, only to be repeated at every step or so. It took me something like half an hour to reach a point within twenty feet of where he lay, and I looked straight into his eyes each time that he stood up.

No wild animal can tell a man from a tree by sight alone if only he stands still. Suddenly, as the cub sprang up, perhaps for the tenth time, there about six feet to one side of him stood the old mother fox. I had not heard a sound or seen a movement, but there she was.

I was so close that I dared not move my head to look at the cub, but turned only my eyes. When I looked back the mother fox was gone. With no sudden movement that I could detect, there almost before my eyes she had melted into the landscape.

I stood like a stone until the cub had lain down once more. This time evidently he was watching me out of his wrinkled-up little eyes, for at my very first forward movement he got up, and with no appearance of haste turned around and disappeared down in the burrow. The watchtower log was vacant, although I have no doubt that the mother fox was watching me from some unseen spot.

When I came to examine the den, I found that there were three burrows in a line, perhaps fifteen feet in length, with a hard-worn path leading from one to the other. The watch log behind them was rubbed smooth and shiny, with reddish fox hairs caught in every crevice. Near the three burrows was a tiny one, which I think was probably dug as an air hole; while in front I found the feathers of a flicker, a purple grackle, and a chicken, besides the remains of the crow aforesaid. How any fox outside of the fable could beguile a crow is a puzzle to me. All of these burrows were in plain sight, and I hunted a long time to find the concealed one, which is a part of the home of every well-regulated fox family. For a while I could find no trace of it. Finally I saw on the side of a stump one reddish hair that gave me a clue. Examining the stump carefully, I found that it was hollow and formed the entrance to the secret exit from the three main burrows.

A week later, I went again to look at the home of that fox family but it was deserted by them and now tenanted by a fat woodchuck, who would never have ventured near the den if the owners had not left it. Mrs. Fox had evidently feared the worst from my visit, and in the night had moved her whole family to some better-hidden home. This was three years ago, and although I visit the place every winter, no telltale tracks ever show that she has moved back.

It is not necessary to go to the forest for adventures; they lie in wait for us at our very doors. My home is in a built-up suburb of a large city, apparently hopelessly civilized. The other morning I was out early for some before-breakfast chopping, the best of all setting-up exercises. As I turned the corner of the garage, I suddenly came face to face with a black-and-white animal with a pointed nose, a bushy tail, and an air of justified confidence. I realized that I was on the brink of a meeting, which demanded courage but not rashness. "Be brave, be brave, but not too brave," should always be the motto of the man who meets the skunk. From my past experience, however, I knew that the skunk is a good sportsman. Unless rushed, he always gives three warnings before he proceeds to extremities.

As I came near, he stopped and shook his head sadly, as if saying to himself, "I'm afraid there's going to be trouble, but it isn't my fault." As I still came on, he gave me danger signal number one by suddenly stamping his forepaws rapidly on the hard ground. Upon my further approach followed signal number two, to wit, the hoisting aloft of his aforesaid long, bushy tail. As I came on more and more slowly, I received the third and last warning—the end of the erect tail moved quietly back and forth a few times. It was enough. I stood stony still, for I knew that if, after that, I moved forward but by the fraction of an inch, I would meet an unerring barrage which would send a suit of clothes to an untimely grave. For perhaps half a minute we eyed each other. Like the man in the story, I made up my mind that one of us would have to run—and that I was that one. Without any false pride, I backed slowly and cautiously out of range. Thereupon the threatening tail descended, and Mr. Skunk trotted away through a gap in the fence into the long grass of an unoccupied lot—probably seeking a breakfast of field mice.

I felt a definite sense of relief, for it is usually more dangerous to meet a skunk than a bear. In fact, all the bears that I have ever come upon were disappearing with great rapidity across the landscape.

But there are times when a meeting with either Mr. or Mrs. Bruin is apt to be an unhappy one. Several years ago, I was camping out in Maine one March in a lumberman's shack. A few days before I came, two boys in a village nearby decided to go into the woods hunting, with a muzzle-loading shotgun and a long stick between them. One boy was ten years old, while the other was a patriarch of twelve. On a hillside under a great bush they noticed a small hole which seemed to have melted through the snow, and which had a gamy savor that made them suspect a coon. The boy with the stick poked it in as far as possible until he felt something soft.

"I think there's something here," he remarked, poking with all his might.

He was quite right. The next moment, the whole bank of frozen snow suddenly caved out, and there stood a cross and hungry bear, prodded out of his winter sleep by that stick. The boys were up against a bad proposition. The snow was too deep for running, and when it came to climbing—that was Mr. Bear's pet specialty. So they did the only thing left for them to do: they waited. The little one with the stick got behind the big one with the gun, which weapon wavered unsteadily.

"Now, don't you miss," he said, " 'cause this stick ain't very sharp."

Sometimes, an attacking bear will run at a man like a biting dog. More often, it rises on its haunches and depends on the smashing blows of its mighty arms and steel-shod paws. So it happened in this case. Just before the bear reached the boys, he lifted his head and started to rise. The first boy, not six feet away, aimed at the white spot which most black bears have under their chin, and pulled the trigger. At that close range, the heavy charge of number six shots crashed through the animal's throat, making a single round hole like a big bullet, cutting the jugular vein, and piercing the neck vertebrae beyond. The great beast fell forward with hardly a struggle, so close to the boys that its blood splashed on their rubber boots. They got ten dollars for the skin and ten dollars for the bounty, and about one million dollars' worth of glory.

Hasting homeward for more peaceful adventures, I find, near the road which leads to the railway station over which scores and hundreds of my friends and neighbors, including myself, pass every day, a little patch of marshland. In the fall it is covered with a thick growth of goldenrod, purple asters, joe-pye weed, wild sunflowers, white boneset, tear thumb, black bindweed, dodder, and a score or more of other common fall flowers.

One night, at nine o'clock, I noticed that an ice blue star shone from almost the very zenith of the heavens. Below her were two faint stars making a tiny triangle, the left-hand one showing as a beautiful double under an opera glass. Below was a row of other dim points of light in the black sky. It was Vega of the Lyre, the great Harp Star. Then I knew that the time had come. We humans think, arrogantly, that we are the only ones for whom the stars shine, and forget that flowers and birds, and all the wild folk are born each under its own special star.

The next morning, I was up with the sun and visited that bit of unpromising marshland past which all of us had plodded year in and year out. In one corner, through the dim grass, I found flaming like deep-blue coals one of the most beautiful flowers in the world: the fringed gentian. The stalk and flower stems looked like green candelabra, while the unopened blossoms showed sharp edges like beechnuts. Above them glowed square fringed flowers of the richest, deepest blue that nature holds. It is bluer than the bluebird's back, and fades the violet, the aster, the great lobelia, and all the other blue flowers that grow. The four petals were fringed, and the flower seemed like a blue eye looking out of long lashes to the paler sky above. The calyx inside was of a veined purple or a silver-white, while four gold-tipped, light purple stamens clustered around a canary-yellow pistil. That morning, I wore on the train one of the two flowers, which I allowed myself to pick. Every friend I met spoke of it admiringly. Some had heard of it, others had seen it for themselves in places far distant. None of them knew that every day until frost they would pass unheedingly within ten feet of nearly thirty of these flowers.

Sometimes the adventure, unlike good children, is to be heard, not seen. It was the end of a hot August day. I had been down for a late dip in the lake, and was coming back through the woods to the old farmhouse where I have spent so many of my summers. The path wound through a grove of slim birches, and the lights in the afterglow were all green and gold and white. From the nearby road, a field sparrow with a pink beak sang his silver flute song; and I stopped to listen, and thought to myself, if he were only as rare as the nightingale, how people would crowd to hear him.

Suddenly, from the depths of the twilight woods, a thrush song began. At first I thought the singer was the wood thrush, which, besides the veery or Wilson thrush, was the only one that I had supposed could be found in that Connecticut township. The song, however, had a more ethereal quality, and I listened in vain for the drop to the harsh bass notes, which always blemish the strain of the wood thrush. Instead, after three arpeggio notes, the singer's voice went up and up, with a sweep that no human voice or instrument could compass, and I suddenly realized that I was in the presence of one of the great singers of the world. For years I had read of the song of the hermit thrush, but in all my wanderings I had never chanced to hear it before.

Lafcadio Hearn writes of a Japanese bird whose song has the power to change a man's whole life. So it was with me that midsummer evening. Some thing had been added to the joy of living that could never be taken from me. Since that twilight I have heard the hermit thrush sing many times. Through the rain in the dawn-dusk on the top of Mount Pocono, he sang for me once, while all around a choir of veerys accompanied him with their strange minor harp chords. One Sunday morning, at the edge of a little Canadian river, I heard five singing together on the farther side. "Ah-h-h, holy, holy, holy," their voices chimed across the still water. In the woods, in migration, I have heard their whisper song, which the hermit sings only when traveling; and once on a May morning, in my back yard, near Philadelphia, one sang for me from the low limb of a bush as loudly as if he were in his mountain home.

No thrush song, however, will ever equal that first one which I heard among the birch trees. Creeping softly along the path that evening, I finally saw the little singer on a branch against the darkening sky. Again and again he sang, until at last I noticed that, when the highest notes were reached and the song ceased to my ears, the singer sang on still. Quivering in an ecstasy, with open beak and half-fluttering wings, the thrush sang a strain that went beyond my range. Like the love song of the bat, perhaps the best part of the song of the hermit thrush can never be heard by any human ear.

It was the morning of June twentieth. I stood at the gate of the farm house where three roads met, and the air was full of birdsongs. For a long time I stood there, and tried to note how many different songs I could hear. Nearby were the altos of the Baltimore oriole. Up from the meadow where the trout brook flowed, came the bubbling, gurgling notes of the bobolink. Robins, wood thrushes, song sparrows, chipping sparrows, bluebirds, vireos, goldfinches, chebecs, indigo birds, flickers, phœbes, scarlet tanagers, red-winged blackbirds, catbirds, house wrens—altogether, without moving from my place, I counted twenty-three different birdsongs and bird notes.

Nearby I saw a robin's nest, curiously enough built directly on the ground on the side of the bank of one of the roads, and lined with white wool, evidently picked up in the neighboring sheep pasture. This started me on another of the games of solitaire, which I like to play out-of-doors, and I tried to see how many nests I could discover from the same vantage point without moving. This is really a good way to find birds' nests, and the one who stands still and watches the birds will often find more than he who beats about. For a long time, the robin's nest was the only one on my list. At last the flashing orange and black of a Baltimore oriole betrayed its gray swinging pouch of a nest in a nearby spruce tree—the only time that I have ever seen an oriole's nest in an evergreen tree. In a lilac bush I saw the deep nest of the catbird, with its four vivid blue eggs and the inevitable grapevine-bark lining around its edge.

In a high fork in a great maple tree at the corner of the road, the chebec, or least flycatcher, showed me her home. Sooner or later, if you watch any of the flycatchers long enough, they will generally show you their nests. This one was high up in a fork, and made of string and wool and down. Over in the adjoining orchard I saw a kingbird light on her nest in the very top of an apple tree; and I have no doubt that, if I had climbed up to it, I would have seen three beautiful cream-white eggs blotched with chocolate-brown.

The last nest of all was my treasure nest of the summer. I was about to give up the game and start off for a walk, when suddenly, right ahead of me, hanging on the limb of a sugar maple, not five feet above the stone wall, I saw the swinging basket nest of a vireo, with the woven white strips of birch bark on the outside, which all vireos use in that part of the country. It was as if a veil had suddenly dropped from my eyes, for I had been looking in that direction constantly, without seeing the nest directly in front of me. Probably, at last, I must have slightly turned my head and finally caught the light in a different direction. I supposed that the nest was that of the red-eyed vireo, the only one of the five vireos which would be likely to build in such a location. Climbing upon the wall to look at it, I saw that the mother bird was on the nest. Even when I took hold of the limb, she did not fly. Then, I slowly pulled the limb down, and still the brave little bird stayed on her nest, although several times she started to her feet and, ruffling her feathers, made as if to fly. As the nest came nearer and nearer, I could see that she was quivering all over with fear, and that her heart was beating so rapidly as to shake her tiny body. Finally, as she came almost within reach of my outstretched hand, she gave me one long look and then suddenly cuddled down over her dearly loved eggs and hid her head inside of the nest. Reaching my hand out very carefully, I stroked her quivering little back. She raised her head and gave me another long look, as if to make sure whether I meant her any harm. Evidently I seemed friendly, for as I stroked her head she turned and gave my finger a little peck, then snuggled her head up against it in the most confiding, engaging way. As she did so, I noticed that a white line ran from the beak to the eye, and that she had a white eye ring and a bluish-gray head. As I looked at her, suddenly from a nearby branch the father bird sang, and I recognized the song of the solitary or blue-headed vireo, who belongs in the deep woods and whose rare nest is usually found in their depths. As the male came nearer, I could see his pure white throat, which with the white line from eye to bill and the greenish-yellow markings on either flank, make good field marks. The four eggs, which I saw afterwards when the mother bird was off the nest, were white with reddish markings all over instead of being blotched at one end, as are those of the red-eyed vireo. Every day for the rest of that week I visited my little friend; and before I left she grew to know me so well that she would not even ruffle up her feathers when I pulled the limb down.

Children are of great help in the life adventurous. They have an inexhaustible fund of admiration for even the feeblest efforts of their parents in adventuring. Many a dull dog, who once heard nothing in all the world but the clank of business, has been changed into a confirmed adventurer by sheer appreciation. Moreover, children possess an energy and imagination, which we grown-ups often lack. Only the other afternoon I started off for a walk with my four, to find myself suddenly dining in the New Forest with Robin Hood, Little John, Will Scarlet, and Allan a' Dale. Owing probably to a certain comfortable habit of person, I was elected to be Friar Tuck.

The forest itself is a wonderful wood of great trees hidden in a little valley between two round green hills. In its centre is a bubbling spring of clear water that never freezes in winter or dries up in summer. That afternoon, we had explored the Haunted House at the edge of the wood, with its date stone of 1809, ten-foot fireplace, and vast stone chimney, and had fearfully approached that door under which a dark stream of blood flowed a half-century ago, on the day when all humans stopped dwelling in that house forever.

Little John climbed puffingly up through two sets of floor beams, to where a few warped hemlock boards still make a patch of flooring in the attic. Under a rafter he found a cunningly concealed hidey-hole, drilled like a flicker's nest into one of the soft mica-schist stones of the chimney. Inside were a battered homemade top, whittled out of a solid block, and two flint Indian arrowheads, ghosts of some long-dead boyhood which still lingered in the little attic chamber.

In the spring twilight we stole out by a side door, so that we might not cross that stained threshold. A lilac bush, which in a century of growth had become a thicket of purple, scented bloom, surrounded the whole side of the house; while beside a squat buttonwood tree of monstrous girth was the dome of a Dutch oven. We followed a dim path fringed with whitethorn and sprays of sweet viburnum blossoms.

From the distance, beyond the farther hill, came the crooning of the toads on their annual pilgrimage back to the marsh where they were born. In time we reached a bank, all blue and white with enameled innocents. In front of this, the campfire was always kindled. The Band scattered for firewood—but not far, for there were too many lurking shadows among those tree trunks. At last, the fire was laid and lighted. Five minutes later, all the powers of darkness fled for their lives before the steady roaring column of smokeless flame that surged up in front of the Band. Followed wassail and feasting galore. Haunches of venison, tasting much like muttonchops, broiled hissingly at the end of green beechwood spits. Flagons of Adam's ale were quaffed, and the loving cup—it was of the folding variety—passed from hand to hand.

All at once, the substantial Tuck heaved himself up to his feet beside the dying fire. There was not a sound in the sleeping forest. Night folk, wood folk, water folk, all were still. Then, from the pursed lips of the Friar sounded a long, wavering, mournful call. Again and again it shuddered away across the hills. Suddenly, so far away that at first it seemed an echo, it was answered. Once and twice more the call sounded, and each time the answer was nearer and louder. Something was coming. As the Band listened aghast, around the circle made by the firelight glided a dark shape with fiery eyes. It realized their worst fears, and with one accord they threw themselves on the Friar, who rocked under the impact.

"Send it back, Fathie, send it back!" they shouted in chorus.

The good Friar unpuckered his lips.

"I am surprised, comrades," he said severely.

"You aren't afraid of an old screech owl, are you?"

"N-n-n-ooo," quavered little Will Scarlet, "if you're sure it's an owl."

"Certain sure," asserted the Friar reassuringly, and gave the call again.

On muffled, silent wings the dark form drifted around and around the light, but never across it, and then alighted on a nearby tree and gave an indescribable little crooning note, which the Friar could only approximate. At last, disgusted with the clumsy attempts to continue a conversation so well begun, the owl melted away into the darkness and was gone. After that, the Band decided that home was the one place for them. Water was poured on the blaze, and earth heaped over the hissing embers. Under the sullen flare of Arcturus and the glow of Algieba, Spica, and all the stars of spring, they started back by dim wood roads and flower-scented lanes. Will Scarlet, Little John, and Allan a' Dale frankly shared the hands of the Friar, and in the darkest places even the redoubtable Robin himself casually took possession of an unoccupied thumb.

II

ZERO BIRDS

It had been a strenuous night. All day the mercury had been flirting with the zero mark, and soon after sunset burrowed down into the bulb below all readings. My bed that night felt like a well-iced tomb. Probably daylight would have found me frozen to death if it had not been for a saving idea. Hurrying into the children's room, I selected two of the warmest and chubbiest. Banking them on either side of me in my bed, I just survived the night. Of course it was hard on them; but then, any round, warm child of proper sentiments should welcome an opportunity to save the life of an aged parent.

In spite of my patent heating plant I woke up toward morning shivering, and remembered with a terrible depression that I had boasted to Mrs. Naturalist and to various and sundry scoffing friends that I would cut down and cut up and haul in one forty-foot hickory tree before the glad New Year. For a while I decided that there was nothing on earth worth exchanging for that warm bed. Finally, however, my better nature conquered, and the dusk before the dawn found me in the woods in front of a dead hickory tree some forty feet high and a couple of rods through—at least that was how its flinty girth impressed me after I had chopped a while. The air was like iced wine. Every axe stroke drove it tingling through my blood.

Before attacking the hickory, however, I began to cut down the brush surrounding the doomed tree, so as to gain clear space for the swing. Almost immediately a vindictive spicebush in falling knocked off my glasses, and they fell into the snow somewhere ahead of me. Without them I am in the same condition as a mole or a shrew, my sense of sight being only rudimentary. Down I plumped on my knees in the snow and fumbled in the half-light with numbed fingers through the cold whiteness ahead.

As I groped and grumbled in this lowly position, suddenly I heard the prelude to one of the most beautiful of winter dawn songs. It was a liquid loud note full of rolling r's. Perhaps it can be best represented in print somewhat as follows: "Chip'r'r'r'r." I forgot my lost glasses and my cold hands and my wet knees waiting for the song that I knew was coming. Another preliminary, rolling note or so, and there sounded from a low stump a wild, ringing song that could be heard for half a mile. "Wheedle-wheedle-wheedle," it began full of liquid bell-like overtones. Then the singer added another syllable to his strain and sang, "Whee-udel, whee-udel, whee-udel." Three times, with a short rest between, he sang the full double strain through, although it was so dark that only the ghostly, black tree trunks could be seen against the white snow. I needed no sight of him, however, to recognize the singer. The song took me back to a bitter winter day in Philadelphia some seventeen years ago, when I was laboriously learning the birds. I was walking through a bit of wasteland encircled by trolley tracks when I heard this same song. It was like nothing which I had ever heard in New England, where I had learned what little I knew about birds, and I searched everywhere for the singer, expecting to see a bird about the size of a robin.

Finally, in the underbrush just ahead of me, I saw an unmistakable wren singing so ecstatically that he shook and trembled all over with the outpouring of his song. It was my first sight and hearing of this southern bird, the Carolina wren, the largest of our five wrens, whose field mark is a long white line over the eye. He is reddish-brown, while the house wren, which is half an inch shorter, is cinnamon-brown. The long-billed marsh wren also has a white line over the eye and is about the same size, but is never found away from the tall grass bordering on water, and has no such song as the Carolina. The winter wren and the short-billed marsh wren could neither of them be mistaken for the Carolina, as both are about an inch and a half shorter and lack the white line. The house wren and the long-billed marsh wren bubble when they sing, the Carolina wren and the winter wren ring, and the short-billed marsh wren, the rarest of all, clicks. Of them all only the Carolina wren sings in the winter.

That day the wren song brought me good luck. It was no more than finished when I heard someone passing along a nearby wood road, who turned out to be an early-rising workman from whom I borrowed some matches with which I finally discovered my missing eyes half buried in the snow. I attacked the pignut hickory with great energy to make up for lost time. Little by little the axe bit through the tough wood, until the kerf was well past the heart of the tree. As I chopped I could hear the quick strokes of a far better woodcutter than I shall ever be. Suddenly he gave a loud, rattling call, and I recognized the hairy woodpecker. He is much larger than the downy, being nearly the size of a robin, while his call is wilder and louder and lacks the downward run of the downy's note. We chopped on together, he at his tree and I at mine. Suddenly from my tree sounded a warning crack, and the trunk wavered for a moment. I stepped well off to one side, for it is dangerous to stand behind a falling tree. If it strikes anything as it falls the trunk may shoot backward. A venerable ancestor of mine, so the story runs, tried to celebrate his ninetieth birthday by chopping down a tree, and standing behind it, was killed by the backlash of the falling trunk.

The tree swayed forward toward the crimson rim of the rising sun. One more stroke at its heart, and there was a loud series of cracks, followed by a roar like thunder as it crashed down. Almost immediately, as if awakened by the noise, I began to hear bird notes. From over to my left sounded a series of sharp, irritating alarm notes, and in the waxing light I caught a glimpse of a crested blood-red bird at the edge of a green-brier thicket. In that same place I had found his nest the spring before, made of twigs and strips of bark and lined with grass and roots and holding three speckled eggs. It was the cardinal grosbeak, another bird unknown to me in New England. No matter how often I meet this crimson-crested grosbeak, he will never become a common bird to me. Each time I see him I feel again something of the thrill which came over me when I first met this singer from the southland in a thicket on the edge of Philadelphia. With the Carolina wren and the tufted titmouse, the cardinal grosbeak completes a trio of birds that can never be commonplace to one born north of Central Park, New York, which is about the limit of their northern range.

Today, as I watched my flaming cardinal, he suddenly dived stiffly into the heart of the thicket. A moment later from its midst sounded a clear, loud whistle, "Whit, whit, whit." I answered him, for this is one of the few birdcalls I can imitate. Before long his dove-colored mate also appeared. Her wings and tail were of a duller red, while the upper parts of her sleek body were of a brownish-ash tint. The throat and a patch by the base of the bill were black in both. As I watched, the singer in the thicket added to his whistle the word "Teu, teu, teu, teu" and then finally ran them together—"Whee-teu, whee-teu, whee-teu," so rapidly whistled that it sounded almost like a single note.

On the way back to breakfast, as the sun came up and warmed a slope of the woods, a flock of slate-colored juncos burst out altogether in a chorus of soft little trills, with now and then sharp alarm notes like the clicking of pebbles together, interspersed with tiny half-whispered notes best expressed by the same letters as those used in writing the grosbeak music—"Teu, teu, teu, teu." Suddenly, from a farther corner of the sun-warmed slope, I heard a few tinkling notes followed by a tantalizing snatch of rich, sweet song shot through with canary-like trills and runs. I hurried over the snow and caught a glimpse of a little flock of birds with crowns of reddish-brown, and each wearing small black spots in the exact centre of their drab-colored waistcoats. They were tree sparrows down from the far North, and I was fortunate to have heard the peculiarly gentle cadence of one of their rare winter songs.

Farther on, the caw of a passing crow drifted down from the cold sky, and before I left the woods I heard the pip of a downy woodpecker and the grunt of the white-breasted nuthatch, that tree climber with the white cheeks which, unlike woodpeckers, can go both up and down trees head-foremost. In the early spring and sometimes on warm winter days, one may hear his spring song, which is "Quee-quee-quee." It is not much of a song, but Mr. Nuthatch is very proud of it and usually pauses admiringly between each two strains. In my early bird days I used to mistake this spring song for the note of an early flicker, and would scandalize better-educated ornithologists by reporting flickers several weeks before their time. The last bird I heard before I left the woods remarked solemnly, "Too-wheedle, too-wheedle, too-wheedle, too-wheedle," like a creaking wheelbarrow, and then suddenly broke out into the flat, harsh "Djay, djay, djay" which has given the silver-and-blue jay its name.

By the time I had reached home, I decided that it was too cold a day to practice law safely. The state legislature in their wisdom had already made the day a half-holiday. Not to be outdone in generosity, I decided to donate my half and make the holiday a whole one. Anent this matter of holidays, the trouble with most of us is that we are obsessed with the importance of our daily work. There are many pleasant byways which we plan to come back and explore when we have reached the end of the straight, steep, and intensely narrow road that leads to achievement. The trouble is that there is no returning. Men die rich, famous, or successful, who have never taken the time to companion their children or to find their way into the world of the wild folk which lies at their very doors. It was not always so. Read in Evelyn's Diary how for sixty years a great man played a great part under three kings and the grim Protector, and yet never lost an opportunity to refresh his life with birdsongs, hilltops, flower fields, and sky air. We reach our goal today in a few desperate years, stripped to the buff like a Marathon runner. One can arrive later and not miss a thousand little happinesses along the way.

With similar arguments I convinced myself on that day, that it was my duty as an amateur naturalist to discover how many birds I could meet between dawn and dark with the thermometer below zero. Certain gentlemen adventurers of my acquaintance aided and abetted me in this plan. They all held high office in a military organization known for short as the Band. There was First Lieutenant Trottie, Second Lieutenant Honey, Sergeant Henny-Penny, and Corporal Alice-Palace, while I had been honored with a captain's commission in this regiment. To be sure, there was something of a dearth of privates; but with such a gallant array of officers their absence was not felt. At any hour of day or night, to the last man, every member of the Band was ready for the most desperate adventures by field and flood.

As we left the house the thermometer stood at four below, while the sky was of a frozen blue, without a cloud, and had a hard glitter as if streaked with frost. In a low tree by the roadside, we heard the metallic note of a downy woodpecker scurrying up the trunk and backing stiffly down. Farther on sounded a loud cawing, and we saw four ruffianly crows assaulting a respectable female broad-winged hawk. One after the other they would flap over her as closely as possible, aiming vicious pecks as they passed. The broad-winged beat the air frantically with her short, wide, fringed wings, and seemed to make no effort to defend herself against her black, jeering pursuers. Once she alighted on an exposed limb. Instantly the crows settled near her and used language which no respectable female hawk could listen to for a moment. She spread her wings and soared away, and as she passed out of sight they were still cawing on her trail.

If the hawk had been one of the swift Accipiters, such as the gray goshawk or the Cooper's hawk, or any of the falcons, no crow would have ventured to take any liberties. One of my friends, who collects bird's eggs instead of bird notes, was once attempting feloniously to break and enter the home of a duck-hawk which was highly regarded in the community—about two hundred feet highly in fact. As my friend was swinging back and forth on a rope in front of the perpendicular cliff, said duck-hawk dashed at him at the rate of some ninety miles per hour. Being scared off by a blank cartridge, the enraged falcon towered. A passing crow flapping through the air made a peck at the hawk as it shot past. That was one of the last and most unfortunate acts in that crow's whole life. The duck-hawk was fairly aching with the desire to attack someone or something which was not protected by thunder and lightning. With one flash of its wings it shot under that misguided crow, and, turning on its back in midair, slashed it with six talons like sharpened steel. The crow dropped, a dead mass of black and blood, to the brow of the cliff below.

Finally we reached the tall, stone chimney—all that is left of some long-forgotten house, which marks the entrance to old Darby Road, which was opened in 1701. At that point Wild Folk Land begins. The hurrying feet of more than two centuries have sunk the road some ten feet below its banks, and the wild folk use its hidden bed like one of their own trails. Foxes pad along its rain-washed course, and rabbits and squirrels hop and scurry across its narrow width, while, in spring and summer, wild ginger, ebony spleenwort, the blue-and-white porcelain petals of the hepatica, and a host of other flowers bloom on its banks. The birds too nest there, from the belted gray-blue and white kingfisher, which has bored a deep hole into the clay under an overhanging wild-cherry tree, down to the field sparrow, with its pink beak and flute song, which watches four speckled eggs close hidden in a tiny cup of woven grass.

Today we followed the windings of the road, until we came to the vast black oak tree which marks the place where Darby Road, after running for nearly ten miles, stops to rest. Beyond stretched the unbroken expanse of Blacksnake Swamp, bounded by the windings of Darby Creek. The Band seated themselves on one of their favorite resting places, a great log which lay under the trees. Above us a white-breasted nuthatch, with its white cheeks and black head, was rat-tat-tatting up and around a half-dead limb, picking out every insect egg in sight from the bark. As the bird came near the broken top of the bough, out of a hole popped a very angry red squirrel exactly like a jack-in-the-box. The red squirrel is the fastest of all the tree-folk among the animals, but a nuthatch on a limb is not afraid of anything that flies or crawls or climbs. He can run up and down around a branch, forward and backward, unlike the woodpeckers, which must always back down, or the brown creepers, which can go up a tree in long spirals but have to fly down.

A red streak flashed down the limb on which the nuthatch was working. That was the squirrel. A fraction of a second ahead of the squirrel there was a wink of gray and white. That was the nuthatch. Before the squirrel could even recover his balance, there was a cheerful rat-tat-tat just behind him on the other side of the limb. As the squirrel turned, the rapping sounded on the other side of the branch. His bushy tail quivered, and using some strong squirrel language, he dived back into his hole. He was hardly out of sight when the nuthatch was tapping again at his door. Once more the squirrel rushed out chattering and sputtering. Once more the nuthatch was not there. Then he tried chasing the bird around the limb, but there was nothing in that. The nuthatch could turn in half the time and space, and moreover did not have to be afraid of falling, for a drop of fifty feet to frozen ground is no joke even for a red squirrel. The aggravating thing about the nuthatch was that, no matter how hard the squirrel chased him, he never stopped for a second, tapping away at the branch, feeding even as he ran. Finally Mr. Squirrel went back to his house and stayed there, while the nuthatch tapped in triumph all around his hole, although muffled chatterings from within expressed the squirrel's unvarnished opinion of that nuthatch.

When the nuthatch finally flew to another tree, we got up and followed a path that twisted through a barren field full of grassy tussocks and clumps of mockernut hickories and black-walnut trees, until it at last lost itself in the depths of Blacksnake Swamp. This swamp had taken its name from the day that we caught a black snake skimming along over the tops of the bushes like a bird. In summer it is full of impassable quagmires, and today we hoped to explore the hidden places which we had never yet seen. We had scarcely passed through the outer fringe of tall grasses and cattails, when we heard everywhere through the cold air little tinkling notes, and caught glimpses of dark sparrow-like birds with forked tails, striped breasts, and streaked rich brown backs, each one showing a fine zigzag whitish line at the bend of the wing. Another field mark was a light patch over each eye, and we identified the first and largest flock of pine siskin of the year. These siskin are strange birds. One never knows when and where they will appear. The last flock that I had seen was in my backyard in May. Usually too they are in trees, and this was the first time that I had ever met with them on the ground. The birds gave little canary-like notes, like goldfinches, which are often found with them, but can always be recognized by their unstreaked breasts and double wing bars.

For a long time we studied the flock through our field glasses, until every last one of the Band had learned this new bird. As we watched them, a white-throated sparrow lisped from a nearby bush, and a little later we met a flock of tree sparrows, a bird which is never by any chance found in a tree. In the distance a woodpecker flew through the air in a labored up-and-down flight, and, as he disappeared, he gave the wild cry of the hairy woodpecker, a bird nearly twice the size of his smaller brother, the downy. Close by the side of the creek, we heard a tiny note like "pheep, pheep, pheep," and, even as we looked for the bird, it flew past and lit on a tree on the other side of the path, not two feet away. We all stood stony still, and in a minute a brown creeper circled the tree, climbing it in tiny hops in a wide spiral. He was so close that we could see his stiff, spiny tail with a little row of spots at its base, and the brown and gray speckles on his back, and his long curiously curved bill.

We pressed on into the very heart of the great, treacherous marsh, today frozen hard and safe, and explored all of its secret places. In a tangle of wild grape vine, we found the round nest, rimmed with grape-vine bark, of the cardinal grosbeak; while over in a thicket of elderberry bushes, all rusty-gold with the clinging stems of that parasite, the dodder, showed the close sheath of the fine branches of a swamp maple. In a fork at the end of one of the branches, all silver-gray, was the empty nest of a goldfinch, the last of all the birds to nest. It was made of twisted strands of the silk of the milkweed pods hackled by the bird's beak. In the snow, we came across a strange track almost like the trail of a snake. It was a wide trough, with little close set, zigzag paw marks running all through it. The Captain told the Band that this was the trail of the fierce blarina shrew, one of the killers. Without eyes or ears, this strange little blind death eats its weight in flesh every twenty-four hours, and slays underground, above ground, and even under the water. The Band regarded the strange tracks with enormous interest.

"How big do they grow?" anxiously inquired Henny-Penny, the littlest but one of the Band.

"Just a little longer than my middle finger," the Captain reassured him.

Suddenly, in the very midst of this zoölogical bric-a-brac, a great thought came to each and every of the Band simultaneously.

"Lunchtime!" they shouted with one accord.

Then occurred the tragedy of the trip. In a pocket of his shooting jacket the Captain had a package of sandwiches containing just one apiece, no more, no less. The rest of the lunch, thick scones, raisins, chocolate, saveloy sausage, bacon, and other necessaries and luxuries, had been wrapped up in another package and intrusted to Honey as head of the commissary department for the day—and Honey had left the package on the hall table! It was a grief almost too great to be borne. The Band regarded their guilty comrade reproachfully. Two large tears ran down Honey's cheeks. Alice-Palace, the littlest of them all, gave way to unrestrained emotions which bade fair to frighten away the most bloodthirsty of blarinas within the radius of a mile.

Then it was that the Captain rose to the emergency. "Comrades," said he, placing one hand over Alice-Palace's widely-opened mouth, "all is not lost. Old woodsmen like ourselves can find food anywhere. Follow me. Hist!"

Like Hawk-Eye and Chingachgook and other well-known scouts, the Captain was apt to employ that mysterious word when beginning a desperate adventure. The Band followed him with entire confidence, albeit with certain snifflings on the part of Corporal Alice-Palace. They crossed a tiny brook, and found themselves in a little grove of swamp maples which had grown up around the fallen trunk of the parent tree. The Captain scanned the trees carefully. Everywhere were trails in the snow which he told them were the tracks of gray squirrels. Suddenly he reached up and picked out from between a little twig and the smooth trunk of a swamp-maple sapling, a big, dry, beautifully-seasoned black walnut. That started the Band to looking, and they found that the little trees were filled with walnuts, each one wedged in between twigs or branches so that it would not blow down. Up and down and about the low trees climbed and scrambled the Band. Some of the nuts were hidden and some were in plain sight, but altogether there was nearly half a peck of them, each one containing a dry, crisp, golden kernel which tasted as rich and delicious as it looked. They had come upon the winter storehouse of a gray squirrel family.

Piling the nuts in the lee of a big oak tree where the campfire was to be made, they followed the Captain to a broken-down rail fence, where grew a thicket of tiny trees with smooth trunks, whose gray twigs were laden down with bunches of what looked like tiny purple plums. Each one had a layer of pulp over a flat stone, and this pulp, what there was of it, had a curious attractive spicy sugary taste. The Captain told the Band that these were nanny plums, sometimes known as sweet viburnum.

Further on, they found clusters of little purple fox grapes, fiercely sour in the fall, but now sweetened enough, under the bite of the frost, to be swallowed.

Still the Captain was not ready to stop. Up the hillside he led them, by a winding path through tangled thickets, until in a level place he brought them to a group of curious trees. The bark of these was deeply grooved and in places nearly three inches thick, while the branches were covered with scores and scores of golden-red globes. Some were wrinkled and frost-bitten until they had turned brown, but others still hung plump and bright in the winter air. It was a grove of persimmon trees. Before he could be stopped, Henny-Penny had picked one of the best looking of the lot and took a deep bite out of the soft pulp. Immediately thereafter he spat out his first taste of persimmon with great emphasis, his mouth so puckered that it was with difficulty that he could express his unfavorable opinion of the new fruit.

"Handsome is as handsome does," warned the Captain. "Try some of the frost-bitten ones."

The Band accordingly did so, and found that the worst-looking and most wrinkled specimens were sweet as honey and without a trace of pucker. On their way back, they passed through a thicket of tangled bushes, whose branches were all matted together in bunches which looked like birds' nests. The twigs were laden down with round, purple berries about the size of a wild cherry, and the Captain told the Band that these were hackberries, otherwise known as sugarberries. They picked handfuls of them, and found that the berry had a sweet spicy pulp over a fragile stone that could be crushed like the stones of a raisin, while the fruit when eaten resembled a raisin in taste.

Hurrying back to the campfire tree, the Captain dug a round circle a couple of feet in diameter in the snow, and spread down a layer of dry leaves. Over these he built a little tepee of tiny, dry, black-oak twigs. Underneath this he placed a fragment of birch bark which he had peeled off one of the aspen birches which grew on the fringe of the swamp. This burned like paper, and in a minute the little ball of dry twigs was crackling away with a steady flame. Over this he piled dry sassafras and hickory boughs, and in a few moments the Band was seated around a column of flame which roared up fully four feet high. With their backs against the great oak tree, they cracked and cracked and cracked black walnuts and crunched sugarberries and nibbled nanny plums and tasted frost grapes—saving the single sandwich until next to the last; while for desert they had handfuls and handfuls of honey-sweet, wrinkled persimmons.

Near the fire Lieutenant Trottie found an old box-cover bedded in the snow. As he lifted it up, there was a rush and a scurry, and from a round, warm nest underneath the cover, made of thistledown, fur, feathers, and tiny bits of wood fiber all matted together into a sort of felt, dashed six reddish-brown, pink-pawed mice. They burrowed in the snow, crept under the leaves, and in a minute were out of sight, all except one, which tried to climb the box cover and which Trottie caught before he could scurry over the top of it. His fur was like plush, with the hair a warm reddish-brown at the ends and gray at the roots. Underneath he was snowy-white, although there, too, the fur showed mouse-gray under the surface. He had little brown claws and six tiny pink disks on each paw, which enabled him to run up and down perpendicular surfaces. His eyes were big and brown and lustrous, and he had flappy, pinky-gray, velvet ears, each one of which was half the size of his funny little face and thin as gossamer. His paws were pink and his long tail was covered with the finest of hairs. When he found he was fairly caught, he snuggled down into Trottie's hand, making a queer little whimpering noise, while his nose wrinkled and quivered. When Trottie brought him to the fire, Henny-Penny offered him a half-kernel of one of his walnuts. Instantly the little nose stopped quivering, and Mousy sat up like a squirrel on the back of Trottie's hand and nibbled away until the piece was all gone. Each one of the Band took turns in feeding him until he could eat no more. Then Trottie put him back in the deserted nest and replaced the box cover.

The last adventure of all was on the way home. We were walking along an abandoned railroad track, when suddenly a flock of light grayish birds flew up all together out of the dry grass and lighted in a small elm tree nearby. As we watched them, they turned and all flew down together. Instantly it was as if a mass of peach blossoms had been spilled on the withered grass and white snow. Fully a third of the flock had crimson crowns and rose-colored breasts, while at the base of the streaked gray-and-brown backs showed a tinge of pink. It was our first flock of the lesser redpolls all the way down from the Arctic Circle. They were restless but not shy, and sometimes we were able to get within six feet of them. They would continually fly back and forth from the tree to the ground, keeping up a soft chattering interspersed with little tinkling notes, somewhat resembling the goldfinch or the siskin which we had left behind us in the swamp. Always, when they flew, they gave a little piping call, and their field mark was a black patch under the throat which could be seen even farther than their red polls or their rosy breasts. Their beaks were light and very pointed, and they had forked tails like the siskin.

It was nearly twilight when we left them and at last started home. As we followed a fox trail in and out through the thickets of Fern Valley, we caught a glimpse of a large brown bird on the ground. At first I thought that it was some belated fox sparrow; but when it hopped to a low twig and then raised its tail stiffly as I watched, I recognized the hermit thrush, which always betrays itself by this curious mannerism. The last one I had seen was singing like Israfel, in the twilight of a Canadian forest. Today the little singer was silent, and I wondered what had kept him back from the southland, and hoped that he would be able to win through the bitter days still ahead of him. I have no doubt that he did, for the hermit thrush is a brave-hearted, hardy, self-reliant bird.

The sun had gone down before we finally reached the road. Above the afterglow showed a patch of apple-green sky against which was etched the faintest, finest, and newest of crescent moons. It almost seemed as if a puff of wind would blow her like a cobweb out of the sky. Above gleamed Venus, the evening star, all silver-gold; while over toward the other side of the sky, great golden Jupiter echoed back her rays. Below the green, the sky was a mass of dusky gold which deepened into amber and then slowly faded. As we walked home through the twilight, we heard the last, sweetest, and saddest singer of that winter day. Through the air shuddered a soft tremolo call, like the whistling of swift, unseen wings or the wail of a little lost child. It was the eerie call of the little screech owl— and never was a bird worse named. Answering, I brought him so close to us that we could see his ear tufts showing in the half-light. All the way home he followed us, calling and calling for someone who will never come.

III

SNOW STORIES

The sun went down in a spindrift of pale gold and gray, which faded into a bank of lead-colored cloud. The next morning, the woods and fields were dumb with snow. No blue jays squalled, nor white-skirted juncos clicked; neither were there any nuthatches running gruntingly up and down the tree trunks. There was not even the caw of a passing crow from the cold sky. As I followed an unbroken wood road, it seemed as if all the wild folk were gone.

The snow told another story. On its smooth surface were records of the lives that had throbbed and passed and ebbed beneath the silent trees. Just ahead of me, the road crossed a circle where, a half-century ago, the charcoal burners had set the round stamp of one of their pits. On the level snow there was a curious trail of zigzag tracks. They were deep and close set, and made by some animal that walked flatfooted. I recognized the trail of the unhasting skunk. Other animals may jump and run and scurry through life, but the motto of the skunk is, "Don't hurry, others will." The tracks of the forepaw, when examined closely, showed long claw marks which were absent from the print of the hind feet. Occasionally, the trail changed into a series of groups of four tracks arranged in a diagonal straight line, which marked where the skunk had broken into the clumsy gallop which is its fastest gait. Most of the time, this particular skunk had walked in a slow and dignified manner. By the edge of the woods he had stopped and dug deeply into a rotten log, evidently looking for winter-bound crickets and grubs.

At this point, another character was added to the plot of this snow story. Approaching at right angles to the trail of the skunk were the tracks of a red fox. I knew he was red, because that is the only kind of fox found in that part of New England. I knew them to be the tracks of a fox, because they ran straight instead of spraddling like a dog, and never showed any mark of a dragging foot. The trail told what had happened. The first tracks were the far-apart ones of a hunting fox. When he reached the skunk's trail, the footprints became close together and ran parallel to the trail and some distance away from it. The fox was evidently following the tracks in a thoughtful mood. He was a young fox, or he would not have followed them at all. At the edge of the clearing, he had sighted the skunk and stopped, for the prints were melted deep into the snow. Sometimes an old and hungry fox will kill a skunk. In order to do this safely, the spine of the skunk must be broken instantly by a single pounce, thus paralyzing the muscles on which the skunk depends for his defense; for the skunk invented the gas attack a million years before the Boche. No living animal can stay within range of the choking fumes of the liquid musk, which the skunk can throw for a distance of several feet. The snow told me what happened next. It was a sad story. The fox had sprung and landed beside the skunk, intending to snap it up like a rabbit. The skunk snapped first. Around the log was a tangle of fox tracks, with flurries and ridges and holes in the snow where the fox had rolled and burrowed. Out of the farther side, a series of tremendous bounds showed where a wiser and a smellier fox had departed from that skunk with an initial velocity of close to one mile per minute. Finally, out of the confused circle came the neat, methodical trail of the unruffled skunk as he moved sedately away. Probably to the end of his life, the device of a black and white tail rampant will always be associated in that fox's mind with the useful maxim, "Mind your own business."

Beyond the instructive fable of the fox and the skunk showed lacework patterns and traceries in the snow where scores and hundreds of the mice folk had come up from their tunnels beneath the whiteness, and had frolicked and feasted the long night through. Some of these tracks were in little clumps of fours. Each group had a five-fingered pair of large prints in front and a pair of four-fingered tracks just behind. Down the middle ran a tail mark. They were the tracks of the white-footed or deer mice. These were the same little robbers which swarmed into my winter camp and gnawed everything in sight. Even a flitch of bacon hung on a cord was riddled with their tiny teeth marks. Only things hung on wires were safe, for their clinging little feet cannot find a footing on the naked iron. One night, they gnawed a ring of round holes through the crown of a cherished felt hat belonging to a friend of mine. The language he used when he looked at that hat the next morning was unfit for the ears of any young deer mouse. Another time, the deer mice carried off about a peck of expensive stuffing from a white horse hair mattress, which I had imported for the personal repose of my aged frame. Although I ransacked that cabin from turret to foundation stone, I could never find a trace of that horse hair. In spite of their evil ways, one cannot help liking the little rascals. They have such bright, black eyes and wear such snowy, silky waistcoats and stockings.

The other evening I sat reading alone in my cabin in the heart of the pine barrens before a roaring fire. Suddenly, I felt something tickle my knee. When I moved, there was a sudden jump and a deer mouse sprang out from my trouser leg to the floor. Then, I put a piece of bread on the edge of the woodbox. Although I saw the bread disappear, I could catch no glimpse of what took it. Finally, I put a piece on my shoe, and after running back and forth from the woodbox several times, Mr. Mouse at last became brave enough to take it. When he found that I did not move, he sat up on my shoe like a little squirrel and nibbled away at his crumb, watching me all the time out of a corner of his black eyes. I forgave him my friend's hat, and was almost ready to overlook the horsehair episode. When I moved, like a flash he dashed up the wall by the fireplace, and hid behind a row of books that stood on the red-oak plank, which I had put in as a mantel piece. Unfortunately, he had forgotten to hide his long silky tail. It hung down through the crack between the plank and the rough stone of the chimney. I tiptoed over and gave it a pinch to remind him to meddle no more with other people's mattresses.

Returning to the wood road—on that morning, among the trails of the deer mice, were the more numerous tracks of the meadow or field mouse. They show no tail mark, and the smaller footprints were not side-by-side as with the deer mice, but almost always one behind the other. These smaller paw marks among all jumping animals, such as rabbits, squirrels, and mice, are always the marks of the forepaws. The larger far apart tracks mark where the hind feet of the jumper come down in front and outside of the fore paws as he jumps.

On that day, among the mouse tracks on the snow, there showed another faint trail, which looked like a string of tiny exclamation marks with a tail mark between them. It was the track of the masked shrew, the smallest mammal of the Eastern states. This tiny fierce fragment of flesh and blood is only about the length of a man's little finger. So swift are the functions of its wee body that when deprived of food for six hours, the shrew starves and dies. Many of them are found starved to death on the melting snow, having crept up from their underground burrows through the shafts made by grass and weed stems. Wandering over the white waste, they lose their way and, failing to find food, starve before the sun is half way down the sky. As the shrew does not hibernate, his whole life is a swift hunt for food; for every day this apparently eyeless, earless animal must eat its own weight in flesh. The weasels kill from bloodlust, but the shrews kill for their very life's sake. It is a fearsome sight to see a shrew attack a mouse. The mouse bites. The shrew eats. Boring in, the shrew secures a grip with its long, crooked, crocodile jaws filled with fierce teeth, and devours its way like fire through skin and flesh and bone, worrying out and swallowing mouthfuls of blood and flesh until the mouse falls over dead. This tiny beastling, the masked shrew, must be weighed by troy weight, and tips a jeweler's scale at less than forty-five grains.

Today, the snow said the shrew had been an unbidden and unwelcome guest at the mice dinner. At first, the mice trails were massed together in a maze of tracks. Where the trail of the shrew touched the circle, there shot out separate lines of mice tracks, like the spokes of a wheel, with the pawmarks far apart, showing that the guests had all sprung up from the laden table of the snow and dashed off in different directions. The shrew track circled faintly here and there, ran for some distance in a long straight trail, and—stopped. The Sword of Damocles, which hangs forever over the head of all the little wild folk, had fallen. The shrew was gone. A tiny fleck of blood and a single track like a great X on the snow told the tale of his passing. All his fierceness and courage availed nothing when the great talons of the flying death clamped through his soft fur. X is the signature of the owl folk, just as K is of the hawk kind. The size of the mark in this case showed that the killer was one of the larger owls. Later in the winter, it might have been the grim white Arctic owl, which sometimes comes down from the frozen North in very cold weather. So early in the season, however, it would be either the barred or the great horned owl.

I had hunted and camped and fished and tramped all through this hill country, and although I had often heard at night the "Whoo, hoo-hoo, hoo, hoo" of the great horned owl, which keeps always the same pitch, I had never heard the call of the barred owl, which ends in a falling cadence with a peculiar deep, hollow note. So, I decided that the maker of the track was that fierce king of the deep woods, whose head, with its ear tufts or horns, may be seen peering from his nest of sticks on the mountainside in a high treetop as early as February. On wings so muffled by soft downy feathers as to be absolutely noiseless, he had swooped down in the darkness, and the tiny bubble of the shrew's life had broken into the void.

Beyond this point, the road wound upward toward the slope of the Cobble: a steep, sharp-pointed little hill, which suddenly thrust itself up from a circle of broad meadows and flat woodlands. Time was when all the Cobble was owned and ploughed clear to its peak by Great-great-uncle Samuel, who had a hasty disposition and a tremendous voice, and ploughed with two yoke of oxen, which required a considerable amount of conversation. Tradition has it that, when discoursing to them, he could be heard in four different towns. That was more than one hundred years ago, and the Cobble has been untouched by plough or harrow since, and today is wooded to the very top.

Just ahead of me on the wood road showed a deep track, which only in recent years has been seen in Connecticut. In my boyhood, a deer track was as unknown as that of a wolf, and the wolves have been gone for at least a century. Within the last ten years, the deer have come back. Last summer I met two on the roads with the cows, and later saw seven make an unappreciated visit to my neighbor's garden, where they seemed to approve highly of her lettuce. Straight up the hillside ran the line of deeply stamped little hoof marks. The trail looks like a sheep's; but the front of each track ends in two beautifully curved sharp points, while the track of a sheep is straighter and blunter. Nor could any sheep negotiate that magnificent bound over the five-foot rail fence. From takeoff to where the four small hoofs landed together on the other side was a good twenty feet.

On the other side of the fence, the snow had drifted over a patch of sweet fern by the edge of the wood road in a low hummock. As I plodded along, I happened to strike this with my foot. There was a tremendous whirring noise, the snow exploded all over me, and out burst a magnificent cock partridge, as we call the ruffed grouse in New England, and whizzed away among the laurels like a lyddite shell. When the snowstorm began, he had selected a cozy spot in the lee of the sweet fern patch, and had let himself be snowed over. The warmth of his body had made a round, warm room, and with plenty of rich fern seeds within easy reach, he was prepared to stay in winter quarters a week, if necessary.

The stories of the snow, although often difficult to read, are always interesting. After the winter fairly sets in, we read nothing about the Seven Sleepers who have put themselves in cold storage until spring. The bear, the raccoon, the woodchuck, the skunk, the chipmunk, and the jumping mouse are all fast asleep underground. The last sleeper never touches the ground when awake, and sleeps swinging upside down by the long, recurved nails on his hind feet. He is the bat who lives and hunts in the air, and can outfly any bird of his own size.

Perhaps the most unexpected of the snow stories was one which I read one winter day when out for a walk with the Botanist. Although the snow was on the ground, the sky was as blue as in June, as the Botanist and I swung into an old road that the forgotten feet of more than two centuries had worn deep below its banks. It was opened in 1691, when William and Mary were king and queen, and Boston Tea Parties and Liberty Bells and Declarations of Independence were not yet even dreamed of in the land.

We always keep a bird record of every walk, and note down the names of the sky folk whom we meet, and any interesting bit of news that they may have for us. In the migration season there is great rivalry as to who shall meet the greatest number from the crowd of travelers going north. Last year, my best day's record was eighty-four different kinds of birds, which beat the Botanist by two. A black duck and a late bay-breasted warbler were the cause of his undoing. To a birdist, every walk is full of possibilities. Any day, anywhere, some bird may flash into sight for the first time.

The Botanist has pointed out to me, not fewer than twenty times, the sacred field where, one bitter winter day, he saw his first (and last) flock of horned larks. For my part, I never fail to show him the pignut hickory where my first golden winged warbler spoke to me one May morning.

Today, however, our walk was almost a birdless one. We heard the caw of the crow, the only bird note that can be certainly counted on for every day of the year. We saw the flutter of the white skirts of the juncos. From a blighted chestnut tree we saw a bird flash down into the dry grass from his perch on a dead limb. As we came nearer, he glided off like a little aeroplane, and we recognized the flight and the spotted buff waistcoat of the sparrow hawk hunting meadow mice.

Later in the morning, we heard the "Pip, pip," of the song sparrow, and marked the black spot on his breast. Far ahead, across a snow-covered meadow, a bird flew dippingly, up and down. He had laid aside his canary-yellow and black suit, but his flight bewrayed the goldfinch.

Passing through a beech wood, we heard a sharp call, and saw a black-and-white bird back down a tree. This cautious procedure stamped him as the downy woodpecker. Of all the tree climbers, only the woodpeckers back down.

Strangely enough, a short distance farther on we heard another cry like that of the downy woodpecker, only harsher and wilder, and caught a glimpse of the hairy woodpecker, the big brother of the downy; a rarer, larger bird of the deep woods. That ended our bird list—a paltry seven when we should have had a score.

We passed the swamp meadow close to the road, where the blue, blind gentian grows not twenty-five yards from the unseeing eyes of the travelers, who pass there every October day and never suspect what a miracle of color lies hidden in the tangle of marsh grass beside their path. The Botanist, with many misgivings, had shown me the secret. For three years we had tramped together before he held me to be worthy to share it.

Farther on, we crossed a plateau where a series of stumps showed where a grove of chestnut trees had grown in the days before the Blight. Suddenly, from under our very feet, dashed a brown rabbit, his white powder puff gleaming at every jump. The lithe, lean, springing body seemed the very embodiment of speed. There are few animals that can pass a rabbit in a hundred yards, even our cottontail, the slowest of his family. He is, however, only a sprinter. In a long distance event, the fox, the dog, and even the dogged, devilish little weasel can run him down.

We looked at the form where he had been lying. It was a wet little hollow made in the dank grass, with only a few dripping leaves for a mattress—a forlorn bed. Yet Runny-Bunny, as some children I know have named him, seems to rest well in his open-air sleeping porch, and even lies abed there.

One far away snowy day in February, two of us stole a few moments from the bedside of a sick child—how long, long ago it all seems now!—and walked out among the wild folk to forget. In a bleak meadow, right at our feet, we saw a rabbit crouched, nearly covered by the snow. He had been snowed under days before, but had slept out the storm until half of his fleecy coverlet had melted away.

He lay so still that at first, we thought he was dead; but on looking closely, we could see the quick throbbing of his frightened little heart. There was not a quiver from his taut body, or a blink from his wide-open eyes. He lay motionless, until my hand stroked gently his wet fur. Then, indeed, he exploded like a brown bombshell from the snow, and we laughed and laughed, the first and last time for many a weary week.

Years later, I was coasting down the meadow hill with one of my boys; and, as the sled came to a stop, a rabbit burst out of the snow, almost between the runners. The astonished boy rolled into a drift, as if blown clear off his sled by the force of the explosion.

Today, as the Brownie sped over the soft snow, we could see how its tracks in series of fours were made. At every jump, the long hind legs thrust themselves far in front. They made the two far apart tracks in the snow, while the close-set fore paws made the nearby tracks. Accordingly, a rabbit is always traveling in the direction of the far apart tracks, quite contrary to what most of us would suppose.

It is the same way with celestial rabbits. Look any clear winter night down below the belt of Orion, and you will see a great rabbit track in the sky—the constellation of Lepus, the Hare, whose track leads away from the Great Dog, with baleful Sirius gleaming green in his fell jaw.

From the rabbit meadow we followed devious paths down through Fern Valley, which in summertime is a green mass of cinnamon fern, interrupted fern, Christmas fern, brake, regal fern, and half a score of others. In the midst of the marsh were rows of the fruit stems of the sensitive fern, which is the first to blacken before the frost. These were heavy with rich wine-brown seedpods, filled with seeds like fine dust. They had an oily, nutty taste; and it would seem as if some hungry mouse or bird would find them good eating during famine times. Yet, so far as I have observed, they are never fed upon.

Along the side of the path were thickets of spicebush, whose crushed leaves in summer have an incense sweeter than burns in any censer of man's making. Today, I broke one of the brittle branches to nibble the perfumed bark, and found at the end of a twig, pretending to be a withered leaf, a cocoon of the prometheus moth. The leaf had been folded together, lined with spun silk, and lashed so strongly that the twig would break before the silken cable.

We passed through a clump of staghorn sumac, with branches like antlers, bearing at their ends heavy masses of fruit clusters made up of hundreds of dark, velvety crimson berries, each containing a brown seed. The pulp of these berries is intensely sour, its flavor giving the sumac its other name of "vinegar plant." These red clusters crushed in sweetened water make a very good imitation of the red circus-lemonade of our childhood. The staghorn is not to be confounded with its treacherous sister, the poison sumac, with her corpse-colored berries. She is a vitriol thrower, and with her death pale bark and arsenic green leaves, always makes me think of one of those haggard, horrible women of the Terror.

It was in Fern Valley that the Botanist made his discovery for the day. It was only a tree, and moreover a tree that he must have passed many times before. Only today, however, did it catch his eye. The bark was that of an oak, but the leaves, which clung thick and brown to the limb, were long, with a straight edge, something like the leaves of the willow oak, only broader and larger. It was no other than the laurel oak, a tree which by all rights belonged hundreds of miles to the south of us.

He walked gloatingly around his discovery, and it was some time before I could drag him on. Thereafter, he gave me a masterly discourse, some forty minutes in duration, on the life history of the oaks, and propounded several ingenious theories to account for the presence of this strange species. This discourse continued until we reached the historic white oak near the end of the valley, where the Botanist once found a flock of bay-breasted warblers in the middle of a rainstorm; again I heard the story of that day.

Through the valley flowed a little stream, and the snow along its banks told of the goings and comings of the wild folk. Gray squirrels, red squirrels, muskrats, rabbits, mice, foxes, weasels, all had passed and repassed along these banks.

To me, the most interesting trail was that of a blarina shrew. His track in the snow is a strange one. It is a round, tunnel-like trail, like that of some large caterpillar, with the trough made by the wallowing little body filled with tiny alternate tracks—one of the strangest of all the winter trails.

I could obtain very little enthusiasm from the Botanist over blarinas. He still babbled of laurel-leafed oaks and similar frivolities. Even the crowning event of the walk left him cold. It came on the homestretch. We were passing through the last pasture before reaching the humdrum turnpike, which led to the tame folk. Suddenly in the snow, I saw a strange trail. It was evidently made by a jumper, but not one whose track I knew. I followed it, until among the leaves in a bank, something moved. Before my astonished eyes hopped falteringly, but bravely, a speckled toad.

The winter sun shone palely on his brown back still crusted with the earth of his chill home. Down under the leaves and the frozen ground he had heard the call, and struggled to the surface, expecting to find spring awaiting him. Two jumps, however, had landed him in a snow bank. It was a disillusion, and Mr. Toad winked his mild brown eyes piteously. He struggled bravely to get out, but every jump plunged him deeper into the snow. His movements became feebler as the little warmth his cold blood contained oozed out.

Just as he was settling despairingly back into the crystallized cold, I rescued him. He was too far gone even to move, for cold spells quick death to the reptile folk. Only his blinking beautiful eyes, like lignite flecked with gold, and the slow throbbing of his mottled breast, showed that life was still in him. He nestled close in my hand, willing to occupy it until warm weather.

I backtracked him from his faltering efforts, and where his first lusty jump showed on the thawing ground I found his hibernaculum. It was only a little hollow, scarcely three inches deep, under sodden leaves and wet earth, and cheerless enough, according to mammalian ideas. It was evidently home for Mr. Toad, and when I set him therein, he scrambled relievedly under some of the loose wet leaves, which had fallen back into his nest. I piled a generous measure of dripping leaves and moist earth over his warted back. It may have been imagination, but I fancied that the last look I had from his bright eyes was one of gratitude. The Botanist scoffed at the idea, for toads, like pine snakes, convey absolutely no appeal to his narrow, flower-bound nature.

I have erected a monument in the shape of a chest-nut stake beside Mr. Toad's winter residence, and I strongly suspect that he will be the last of his family to get up when the spring rising-bell finally rings.

"There's positively nothing to this early rising business," I can hear him telling his friends at the Puddle Club in April. "Look at what happened to me. If it hadn't been for a well-meaning giant, I would have caught my death of cold from getting out of bed too soon. Never again!"

Our calendar makers use red letters to mark special days. Personally, I prefer orchids and birds and sunrises and nests and snakes and similar markers. I have in my diary "The Day of the Prothonotary Warbler," "The Day of the Henslow's Sparrow's Nest" (that was a day!), "The Day of the Fringed Gentian," and many, many others. But, always and forever, that snowy 21st of December is marked in my memory as "The Day of the Early Toad."

Once more, I was climbing the Cobble. The wood road on which I started had narrowed to a path. Overhead, masses of rock showed through the snow, and above them were the dark depths of the Bear Hole, where Great-great-uncle Jake had once shot with his flintlock musket the largest bear ever killed in that part of the state. It was here at the cliff side that Shahrazad snow told me another story.

Along the edge of the slope ran a track made up of four holes in the snow. The front ones were far apart and the back ones near apart. Occasionally, instead of four holes, five would show in the snow, and the position of the marks was reversed. A little farther on, and the trail changed. The two near apart tracks were now in a perpendicular line instead of side by side. To Chingachgook, or Deerslayer, or Daniel Boone, or any other well-known tracker, the trail would have, of course, been an open book. But, it had taken an amateur trailer like myself some years to be able to read that snow record aright. The trail was that of a cottontail rabbit. At first he had been hopping contentedly along, with an eye open for anything eatable in the line of winter vegetables. The far apart tracks were the paw marks of the big hind legs, which came in front of the marks made by the fore paws as they touched the ground at every hop. The five marks were where he had sat down to look around. The fifth mark was the mark of his stubby tail, and when he stopped, the little fore paws made the near apart marks in front of the far apart marks of his hind feet, instead of behind them as when he hopped.

Suddenly, the rabbit detected something alarming coming from behind, for the sedate hops changed into startled bounds. A little farther on the trail said that the rabbit had caught sight of its pursuer as it ran; for a rabbit by the position of its eyes sees backward and forward equally well. The tracks showed a frantic burst of speed. In an effort to get every possible bit of leverage, the fore legs were twisted so that they struck the ground one behind the other, which accounted for the last set of marks perpendicular to those in front. A line of tracks, which came from a pile of stones, and paralleled the rabbit's trail, told the whole story. The pawmarks were small and dainty, but beyond each pad print were the marks of fierce claws. No wonder the rabbit ran wild when it first scented its enemy, and then saw its long slim body bounding along behind, white as snow except for the black tip of its tail.

It was the weasel, whose long body moves like the uncoiling of a steel spring. A weasel running looks like a gigantic inchworm that bounds instead of crawls. Speed, however, is not what the little white killer depends on for its prey. It can follow a trail by scent better than any hound, climb trees nearly as well as a squirrel; and if the animal it is chasing goes into a burrow, it has gone to certain death. The rabbit's only chance would have been a straightaway run at full speed for miles and hours. In this way it could probably have tired out the weasel, which is a killer, not a runner, by profession. A rabbit, however, like the fox, never runs straight. Round and round in great circles it runs about its feeding ground, of which it knows all the paths and runways and burrows. Against a dog or fox, these are safer tactics than exploring new territory. Against a weasel, they are usually fatal.

It was easy to see on the snow what had happened. At first, when the rabbit saw the weasel looping along its trail like a hunting snake, it had started off with a sprint that in a minute carried it out of sight. Then a strange thing happened. Although a rabbit can run for an hour at nearly top speed, and in this case had every reason to run, after a half mile of rapid circling and doubling, the trail changed and showed that the rabbit was plodding along as if paralyzed.

One of the weird and unexplained facts in nature is the strange power that a weasel appears to have over all the smaller animals. Many of them simply give up and wait for death when they find that a weasel is on their trail. A red squirrel, which could easily escape through the treetops, sometimes becomes almost hysterical with fright, and has been known to fall out of a treetop in a perfect ecstasy of terror. Even the rat, which is a cynical, practical animal, with no nerves, and a bitter, brave fighter when fight it must, loses its head when up against a weasel. A friend of mine once saw a grim, gray old fellow run squealing aloud across a road from a woodpile and plunge into a stone wall. A moment later, a weasel in its reddish summer coat came sniffing along the rat's trail and passed within a yard of him.

This night, the rabbit, with every chance for escape, began to run slowly and heavily as if in a nightmare, watching the while its back trail. And when the weasel came in sight again, the trail stopped as the rabbit crouched in the snow, waiting for the end. It came mercifully quick. When the weasel saw the rabbit had stopped, its red eyes flamed, and with a flashing spring its teeth and claws were at poor bunny's throat. There was a plaintive whinnying cry, and the reddened snow told the rest.

So the last story of the snow ended in tragedy, as do nearly all true stories of the wild folk. Yet, they need not our pity. Better a thousand times the quick passing at the end of a swift run or of a brave fight, than the long, long weariness of pain and sickness by which we humans so often claim our immortality.

IV

A RUNAWAY DAY

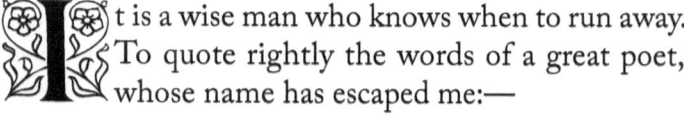t is a wise man who knows when to run away. To quote rightly the words of a great poet, whose name has escaped me:—

> He who works and runs away
> May live to work another day.

So it was that, like Christian of old, I suddenly decided to escape for my life from my city.

There were many reasons. It was a holiday. Then the sun rose on one of the most perfect days that ever dawned since the calendar was invented. Furthermore, there was the thought of a little cabin hidden in the heart of the pine barrens. So I ran away through snow-covered meadows and silent woods and past farmhouses that were old when this republic was first born, until my law offices and the city and the noise and the dust and the smoke were all behind the horizon.

An hour later I was following a little path that zig-zagged back and forth through thickets of scrub oak and stiff rows of pitch pines. Above the trees was the rush of wings. The upper air was filled with the victorious sound of going that heartened David from the tops of the mulberry trees in that dread valley of Rephaim. Perhaps it was the wind; but why did not the treetops sway instead of standing in frozen rows? The sky above was the color of the eggs of the wood thrush, a tender blue faintly washed with white. As the sun rose higher and higher, the color deepened to that bluest of blues which burns in May under the breast of the brooding catbird. Filtered through frost, the sunlight shone, intensely bright but without heat. The air was full of the spicery of a million pine trees. With every breath it went tingling through my blood, carrying with it the joy of the open and the freedom of the barrens.

At last I came to the cabin. It is set on the very edge of the brownest, crookedest, sweetest stream in the world—the cedar-stained Rancocas. The wide porch overhangs the water, and over the doorway is a tiny horseshoe, which was dug out of the bog at Upper Mill, undoubtedly cast by some fairy steed. One whole side of the cabin is taken up by an arched fireplace built of brown and yellow and red sandstone, the only stone that can be found in the Barrens. Squat and curly, two massive andirons, hammered out of bog iron, stand among the ashes. They have a story all their own.

Five miles through the woods is Upper Mill, which is not a mill at all, but marks the place where, a century ago, one stood. The only occupied house there is a log cabin built of imperishable white-cedar logs in 1720, the date still showing on one of the logs. Charlie Rogers lives there alone. It used to be an old tavern on the cattle road from Perth Amboy. Every now and then Charlie finds old coins, King George III pennies and farthings, and the rare New Jersey pennies which were coined only during two years, and which bear a plough and the old name of New Jersey—Nova Cæsarea. One day, when I was gossiping with Charlie, I told him that, if he took up the old dirt floor and sifted it through an ash sifter during the long winter evenings, he might find a further store of rare coins. He took my advice, and the first treasure he uncovered was these andirons buried where once had been a hearth. Charlie gave them to me, and they hold up logs now as well as they did two hundred years ago.

As I slipped into a well-worn suit of khaki, all the worry of the month fell off my shoulders and rolled down the bank and was drowned in the golden water. Tucking a pair of field glasses into one pocket and a package of lunch into the other, I started off on an exploring trip. In the barrens everywhere are paths that wind for miles in and out among the trees and along the edges of brooks and bogs. Who made them? Who keeps them open? No one knows. I have been able to follow a few of them out to the end. One leads to Ong's Hat, a little clearing in the heart of the woods, where grows an enormous white oak tree. A century and a half ago Ong, the Indian, lived there. One day he disappeared. Nothing was ever found except his blood-stained hat. Then there is the path that leads to Sheep-Pen Hill, where seven empty houses and a well stand deserted and alone. Others lead to Gum Sprung, which, being translated, means Gum-Tree Cove, and to Double Trouble and Mount Misery, where the rattlesnake den is, and Apple-Pie Hill, and Friendship, and a host of other places that I have not explored.

Today I walked for miles and miles through stretches of low, gleaming pines and past pools set in golden sphagnum moss. The wind had died down, and the silence seeped in and carried with it the comfort of the wilderness. The first friend I met was a little bird that dived like a mouse into a pile of brush. I saw a brook, and hurried to it, knowing that if the bird were a winter wren it could not possibly keep from running along the edges of that brook. Sure enough, in a minute I saw it darting in and out of holes and with cocked tail curtsying on the stones. It is the next to the smallest of our five wrens—only the rare short-billed marsh wren is tinier.

Today all through the treetops I heard the high-pitched tiny notes of that tiny bird, the golden-crowned kinglet. Its forked tail, striped head, and wing bars are the field marks by which it can be told in spite of its quick movements. It is the third smallest of all our birds: only the hummingbird and the short-billed marsh wren are smaller. Beyond the kinglet I heard the clicking alarm notes and saw a flutter of the white skirts of a junco as it flew up ahead of me, showing its white tail feathers, while in the woods a silver-and-blue bird sprang out of the bushes, for a wonder without a sound. It was the blue jay, which scolds and squalls all day long. Overhead, in spite of the bitter cold, the grim black buzzards, with their fringed wings and black-and-gray undersides, wheeled in the air, while the smaller crow flapped laboriously beneath them.

Near a stream I came upon a patch of the rare climbing fern, an evergreen fern which climbs like a vine and has flat, veined leaves that look like little green hands with four and five fingers. The stem is like drawn copper wire. Beyond the fern I met the pale-gray poison sumac, with its corpse-colored berries growing out from the sides of the twigs instead of from the end, as do the berries of the harmless varieties.

I followed Pond-Lily Path through the white sand that in the springtime is all golden with barrens heather. It winds in and out through the scattered clumps of low pitch pine and thickets of scrub oak, and finally leads to a still brook all afloat in midsummer with pond lilies. When the path reached the bogs, which today were frozen solid, I turned in, crossing them on the snow-covered ice. Everywhere were lines of four-toed crow tracks, and here and there were rabbit trails, a series of four round holes in the snow.

The next morning, when I followed my own tracks, I found that for more than a mile I had been trailed by some animal making a series of little paw prints like those of a small cat, except that they were close together and sometimes doubled, showing where the animal had given sudden bounds. It was none other than the trail of a weasel, probably the long-tailed variety, although that is rare in the barrens. Like others of his family, this animal often follows a man's tracks for a long distance, perhaps out of curiosity, perhaps in the hope of finding food. As I looked at the trail of this little killer, I was glad that he was not larger. If weasels, or those other killers, the shrews, were as large as a dog, no man's life would be safe out of doors.

I explored so far that the sun had set before I turned back for the cabin. Suddenly, from far over where the tree trunks were inked black against the golden afterglow. I heard a hoot, deep rather than loud. "*Hoo, hoo-hoo, hoo, hoo!*" it went, and sometimes. "*Hoo-hoo-hoo!*" Usually, though, the second note was doubled. It meant that the great horned owl with its speckled gray back and white collar was hunting rabbits through the silent woods. If it had been the barred owl, the third note would have been doubled and the last note would have had a drop in its cadence.

In the frosty twilight I hurried along the winding path, back to the cabin and a long, dreamy evening before the roaring fire. First came a wonderful exhibition of free-hand cooking. Then I piled the great fireplace well up the chimney with masses of pitch-pine knots and stumps that I had dug up in the dry bogs. All of the sapwood had decayed., leaving nothing except the resinous bones of the fallen trees. They burned at the touch of a match, with a red smoky flame. Above them

I banked dry lengths of swamp maple and post oak. Then, drawing up a vast rocker well within the circle of the heat. I settled down to read and dream in front of the red coals.

There is nothing in life sweeter than a little loneliness. Nowadays we live and die in crowds, like ants and bees, so that solitude is likely to become one of the lost arts. No book ever tastes so well as before a great fire in the heart of a wilderness, even if the wilderness be only a few miles away. In my cabin I keep a special shelf of the books which I have always wanted to read, and for which in some way I never find time in the hurry of everyday life. That evening I sat for long over the Saga of Burnt Njal, and read again of the bill of Gunnar and the grim axe, the "ogress of war," of Skarphedinn and the sword of the dauntless Kari. In the flickering firelight I pictured the death fight of Gunnar of Lithend, one of the four great fights of one man against a multitude in history, and heard again Hallgarda, the fair and the false, forsake him to his death.

"Give me two locks of thy hair," said Gunnar to Hallgarda, when that his bowstring was cut in twain; "and ye two, my mother and thou, twist them together into a bowstring for me."

"Does aught lie on it?" she says.

"My life lies on it," he said.

"I will not do it," said Hallgarda; "for know ye now that I never cared a whit for thee."

At last it was time to go to bed. I went out to get a drink of the most wonderful water in the world. Near the cabin a little bog was frozen over a foot deep with white bubbled ice. In one place a round, black hole had betrayed the secret spring that flooded the whole swale. In the coldest weather this spring hole remains unfrozen. I dipped up a pitcher full of the soft, spicy cedar water pulsing from the very heart of the marsh. The Pinies have a saying that he who drinks cedar water will always come back to the barrens, no matter how far afield he may wander.

As I came to the porch steps, in the dark stream just below me I saw a strange thing. Underneath the water a ball of fire flashed down the stream and disappeared around the bend. For a long time I tried to puzzle out what it could be. There was no form of aquatic phosphorescent life that would swim through a northern stream in the depths of winter. It was only when I started to tell the time by the sky clock that the mystery was solved. I was looking at the star Caph in Cassiopeia, which is the hour hand of the clock, when suddenly a meteor flashed down the sky, and I realized that my submarine of a few moments before had been only the reflection of another shooting star.

As I stopped on the porch with my pitcher, the open door made a long lane of light. Just across the creek, not fifty feet away, sounded a crash in the brush, and there in the spotlight, held by the glare, stood a big buck. For a moment I looked right into his beautiful, liquid, gleaming eyes. Then, with a snort, he plunged into the woods and was gone. For years I had tramped through the barrens and had found the tracks of the deer that still live not thirty miles from the third largest city in America, but until that night I had never seen one.

It grew colder and colder, and the little cabin snapped and cracked with the frost. Banking up the fireplace with logs, I pulled my bed up into the circle of heat, and fell asleep to the flickering of the fire and the croon of the wind among the pine trees outside. Through the window I could see the winter sky ablaze with stars, while the late moon shone like a bowl of frozen gold through the black tree trunks.

The next morning I had to leave on the nine-o'clock train; and so I rose early and after breakfast took a last walk down to Lower Mill and back, to see if I could add any more winter birds to my list. It was a cold, clear, snapping winter morning, and as the sun came up through the pine trees I met first one and then another of the bird folk abroad after their breakfasts. First I heard the "Pip, pip!" of the downy woodpecker, all black and white, with a bloodstain at the back of his head. He is a tree climber who can go up a tree head-foremost, but must always back down. The nuthatches, with their white cheeks and grunting notes, can go up and down a tree either head first or tail first and the last of the tree climbers, the brown creeper, climbs up in a spiral, but has to fly down.

Farther on, I heard the call of the big hairy wood-pecker, which looks almost like the downy except that he is nearly twice as large. He was drilling a hole in the underside of a branch and sucking out hibernating ants with his long, sticky trident tongue. Next came a tree sparrow, with his white wing bar and brown-red patch on the crown of his head. He was busily scratching on the ground; he is called a tree sparrow because never by any chance is he found in a tree. On the side of a white oak tree a bit of bark seemed to move upward in a spiral, and I recognized the brown creeper, the last of the climbers. He went up the tree in a series of tiny hops and then, true to his training, flew down and started up again.

As I turned the curve by Lower Mill, I saw in a thicket near the dam a number of white-throated sparrows, with their striped white heads and white throat patches. Near them suddenly hopped a bird that ought to have been far south. It was reddish brown with a long tail, and I recognized the female chewink. She hopped around and scratched among the leaves like a little hen, in true chewink style, as if the month were April instead of January.

I hurried around a bend in the road and heard over my head a series of loud *pips*, much like the note of an English sparrow. I looked up—and there was my great adventure. A little locust tree was filled with a flock of plump, large birds. At first I thought that they were cedar birds, but in a moment I caught sight of their coloring. Six of the males out of the flock of seventy-four were in full plumage. Their forked tails were velvet black. Their wings were the golden white of old ivory, with a broad black edge, their heads grayish black, and their breasts and backs a deep, rich gold; and, strangest of all, their thick beaks were of a greenish-white color.

It was a great moment. For the first time in my life I had met the evening grosbeaks, and had found what afterwards proved to be the largest flock ever reported of this rare bird of the far north so far south. For a delightful hour I followed them. They were restless, but not shy. Sometimes they alighted on the ground and then flew up all together, like a flock of starlings. They looked like overgrown goldfinches, just as the pine grosbeak looks like an overgrown purple finch, and the blue grosbeak of the south for all the world like a monstrous indigo bunting. As I followed them, suddenly I heard a sharp *chip*, and to my delight there flashed into sight the crested cardinal grosbeak, blood-red against the snow. For a moment the lithe, nervous, flaming bird of the south met its squat, strong, stolid cousin of the far north.

I could come quite near without alarming them, and then suddenly they would all fly away together to some other tree without any apparent reason. Besides the sparrow-like note that I first heard, they had a sort of trilling chirp. Once they all started like a flock of goldfinches or grackles in a chirping chorus. When they flew, they sometimes gave a single, clear flight note, but never made a sound when feeding on the ground. The birds had short, slightly forked tails, and the yellow ring around the eye gave them, when seen in profile, a curious spectacled appearance; while the huge beak and short tail made them seem clumsy as compared with the other grosbeaks. The plumage of the females showed mottled black-and-white wings and greenish-yellow backs and breasts. The iris of the eye in both sexes was red, the legs of a bluish-gray pink, and the feet of a grayish-pink color.

Later I found that the birds fed on the berries of the poison ivy, red cedar, climbing bittersweet, and the buds and embryo needles of the pitch pine, together with the seeds of the box elder. The favorite food of the flock that I watched seemed always to be the pits of the wild black cherry (*Prunus serotina*). They would take the pits well out of sight back into their beaks, keeping their bills half open in a comical manner, as if they had a bone in the throat. A second later there would be a cracking noise and out would drop two nicely split segments of the cherry pits, the meat having been swallowed. Sometimes in the trees they would sidle along the limbs exactly as a parrot does along its perch.

The authorities state that the evening grosbeak has no immature plumage, but passes after its first molting immediately into full plumage. I saw one, however, that I am sure was in immature plumage. The back was yellowish instead of being gray, like the females', and the wings were of a dirty white color instead of being mottled black and white, like the plumage of the females, or half black and half white, like the plumage of the males. Both sexes seemed to have the same call and gave it equally often.

The history of the evening grosbeak illustrates the far-reaching and never-ending consequences of a falsehood. This bit of moralizing is called forth because of the name of this sorely misdescribed bird. In three languages,

English, Greek and Latin, the myth is perpetuated that the evening grosbeak, or *Hesperiphona vespertina vespertina*, sings only at twilight. It all began in 1823, when one Major Delafield, a boundary agent of the United States government, was camping northwest of Lake Superior. There he met a flock of evening grosbeaks in the twilight, and instantly jumped to the conclusion that the birds were accustomed to spend the day in the dark recesses of impassable swamps and come out and sing only at evening.

As a matter of fact, the evening grosbeak goes to bed at dark, like all other respectable, reputable birds. Its song is a wandering, jerky warble that the singer himself recognizes as a miserable failure, for he often stops and looks discontented and then remains silent for a minute before trying again. It sounds like the early part of a robin's song, but is always suddenly checked as if the performer were out of breath. The guess of the imaginative major was later elaborated by Prince Lucien Bonaparte, Nuttall, and even by later ornithologists,—Coues among them,—not one of whom had ever seen or heard the bird. Coues's description in his "Key to North American Birds" is worth quoting as a specimen of the rhetoric in which a past generation of ornithologists dared to indulge.

> A bird of distinguished appearance, whose very name suggests the faraway land of the dipping sun and the tuneful romance which the wild bird throws around the close of day. Clothed in striking color contrast

of black, white and gold, he seems to represent the allegory of diurnal transmutation, for his sable pinions close around the brightness of his vesture, as night encompasses golden hues of sunset, while the clear white space enfolded in these tints foretells the dawn of the morrow.

That morning I knew nothing of the history or the habits of this unknown and misrepresented bird. All I knew was that for me the twenty-ninth day of January, 1917, would be marked in my calendar forever by a bird from the north, all dusky gold and velvet black and ivory white—the Day of the Evening Grosbeak.

At last the time came to leave them. As I started back for home, the sun showed through the trees like a vast red coal, with a smoke of clouds drifting across its face, and I traveled back to town in the full glory of a clear winter morning, filled with the measureless content of a great discovery. It was good to be alive and to look forward to more work and to more glorious, adventure-filled runaway days.

V

THE RAVEN'S NEST

After all, the Rosicrucians were an ignorant lot. They spent their days over alembics, cucurbits, and crucibles—yet they grew old. In our days many men—and a few women—have discovered the Elixir of Youth—but never indoors. The prescription is a simple one. Mix a hobby with plenty of sky air, shake well, and take twice a week. I know a railroad official who retired when he was seventy. "He'll die soon," observed his friends kindly. Instead, he began to collect native orchids from all points of the compass. Now, he is too busy tramping over mountains and through woods and marshes even to think of dying. Anyway, he would not have time until he has found the ram's head and the cranesbill orchids and finished his monograph on the *Habenaria*. He will never grow old.

Neither will that other friend of mine, who collects fresh-water pearls, nor the one who makes me visit black snake and rattlesnake dens with him every spring, nor those others who spend their time in collecting butterflies, beetles, wasps, and similar bric-a-brac. As for those four abandoned oölogists who have hunted with me for years, they will be young at a hundred. They rank high in their respective callings. Yet, from February, when the great horned owl begins its nest, until the goldfinch lays her white eggs in July, the four spend every holiday and vacation hunting birds' nests.

Personally, I collect only notes, out-of-door secrets, and little everyday adventures. Birdsongs, flower fields, and friendships with the wild folk mean far more to me than cabinets of pierced eggs, dried flowers, stuffed birds, and tanned skins. Nor am I much of a hunter. When it comes to slaughtering defenseless animals with high-powered guns, I prefer a position in an abattoir. One can kill more animals in a day, and with less exertion. Yet my collecting and sporting friends make allowances for my vagaries and take me with them on their journeyings. Wherefore it happened that in early March I received a telegram: "Raven's nest located. Come if you are man enough."

Now, a middle-aged lawyer and the father of a family has no business ravening along the icy and inaccessible cliffs, which that gifted fowl prefers for nursery purposes. I have, however, a maxim of Thoreau, which I furbish up for just such occasions. "A man sits as many risks as he runs," wrote that wanderer in the woods. Accordingly, the next morning found me two hundred miles to the north, plodding through a driving snow storm toward

Seven Mountains, with the first man in recent years to find the nest of a northern raven in Pennsylvania.

For fifteen freezing miles we clambered over and around three of the seven. By the middle of the afternoon, we reached a cliff hidden behind thickets of rhododendron. In the meantime, the snow had changed to a lashing rain, probably the coldest that has ever fallen on the North American continent. Ploughing through slush, the black rhododendron stems twisted around us like wet rubber, and the hollow green leaves funneled ice water down our backs and into our ears. Breaking through the last of the thickets, we at length reached a little brook, which ran along the foot of the cliff. A hundred feet above, out from the middle of the cliff, stretched a long tongue of rock. Over this the cliff arched like a roof, with a space between which widened toward the tip of the tongue. In a niche above this cleft, a dark mass showed dimly through the rain.

"The nest!" muttered the Collector hoarsely, pouring a pint or so of rain water down my neck from his hat brim as he bent toward me. I stared with all my eyes, at last one of the chosen few to see the nest of a Pennsylvania raven. It was made of large sticks. The fresh broken ends and the droppings on the cliff side showed that it was a recent one. There were no signs of either of the birds. We solemnly removed our coats and sweaters and prepared for the worst. To me, the cliff looked much like the Matterhorn, only slipperier. The Collector, however, was most reassuring. He told me that the going looked worse than it really was, and that, anyway, if I did fall, death would be so nearly instantaneous as to involve little if any suffering.

Thus encouraged, I followed him gruntingly up a path, which had evidently been made by a chamois, or an ibex. At last, I found myself perched on a shelf of stone about the width of my hand. The Collector, who was above me on an even smaller foothold, took this opportunity to tell me that the rare Allegheny cave rat was found on this cliff, and nearly fell off his perch trying to point out to me a crevice where he had once seen the mass of sticks, stones, leaves, feathers, and bones with which these versatile animals barricade their passage-ways. I refused to turn my head. That day, I was risking my life for ravens, not rats. Above us was the long, rough tongue of rock. Below us, a far hundred feet, the brook wound its way through snow-covered boulders.

Again, the Collector led the way. Hooking both arms over the tongue of rock above him, he drew himself up until his chest rested on the edge, and then, sliding toward the precipice, managed to wriggle up in some miraculous way without slipping off. From the top of the tongue he clambered up to the niche where the nest was, calling down to me to follow. Accordingly, I left my shelf and hung sprawlingly on the tongue; but there was no room to push my way up between it and the rock-roof above.

"Throw your legs straight out," counseled the Collector from above, "and let yourself slide."

I tried conscientiously, but it was impossible. My sedentary, unadventurous legs simply would not whirl out into space. At last, under the jeers of my friend, I shut my eyes and, kicking out mightily, found myself sliding toward eternity. Just before I reached it, under the Collector's bellowed instructions, I thrust my left arm up as far as I could, and found a handhold on the slippery rock. After getting my breath, I managed to wriggle up through the crevice and lay safe on the top of the tongue. The niche above was not large enough for us both, so the Collector came down while I took his place. I was lashed by a freezing rain, my numb hands were cut and bleeding, and there were ten weary miles still ahead. Yet that moment was worth all that it cost. There is an indescribable fascination and triumph in sharing a secret with the wild folk, which can be understood only by the initiate. The living naturalists who had looked into the home of the Northern raven in Pennsylvania could be counted on the thumb and first three fingers of one hand. At last the little finger belonged to me.

The deep cup of the nest was about one foot in diameter and over a yard across on the outside. It was firmly anchored on the shelf of rock, the structure being built into the crevices and made entirely of dead oak branches, some of them fully three quarters of an inch in diameter. It looked, from a distance, like an enormous crow's nest. The cup itself was some six inches deep, and lined with red and white deer hair and some long black hairs, which were probably those of a skunk. Inside, it had a little damp green moss; while the rim was made of green birch twigs bruised and hackled by the beaks of the builders. On this day, March 9, 1918, there were no eggs, although in a previous year, the Collector had found two as early as February 25, when the cliffs were covered with snow; and on March 5 of another year he collected a full set of five fresh eggs, which I afterwards examined in his collection. The birds had built a nest the year before, without laying. This fact, with the absence of eggs this year, convinced the Collector that the birds were sterile from age. During the last years of their long life, which is supposed to approach a century, a pair of ravens will sometimes build, with pathetic pains, nest after nest, which are never occupied by eggs. The Collector promised to show me a set, however, the next day in another nest.

At last it was time to start down. The Collector, who was waiting on his shelf, warned me that the descent was more difficult than the climb which I had just lived through, as it was necessary to slide some six feet backwards to the shelf from which we started. As I looked down the cliffside, I decided to remain with the ravens. It was not until the Collector promised most solemnly to catch me, that I at last let go and found myself back on the shelf with him. Then came another wonderful moment. "Crrruck, crrruck, crrruck," sounded hoarsely from the valley below—a note like that of a deep-voiced crow with a bad cold.

"Hurry!" urged the Collector; "it's one of the old birds coming back.

"I claim to have hurried as much as any man of my age could be expected to do, but by the time I had reached the path, the wary raven had disappeared. I clambered down the cliff while the Collector reproached me for my senile slowness. We stopped to rest at the foot, and I was just telling him that the Cornishmen hate the raven because to their ears he always cries "Corpse, corpse!" when suddenly the bird itself came back again. It flew across the valley and alighted on a tree top by the opposite cliff, looking like a monster crow, being about one-third longer. One might mistake a crow for a raven, but never a raven for a crow. If there be any doubt about the bird, it is always safe to set it down as a crow.

The flight of the raven, which consisted of two flaps and a soar, and its long tail resembling that of an enormous grackle, were its most evident field marks.

For long, we sat and watched the wary birds, until, chilled through by the driving rain, we started to cover the ten miles that lay between us and the house of Squire McMahon, a mountain friend of the Collector, where we planned to pass the night. On the way, the Collector told me that he saw his first raven while wandering through the mountains in the spring of 1909, and how he trailed and hunted and watched until, in 1910, he found the first nest. Since then he had found twelve. His system was a simple one. Selecting from a gazetteer a list of mountain villages with wild names, such as Bear Creek, Paddy's Mountain, and Panther Run, he would write to the postmasters for the names of noted hunters and woodsmen. From them, he would secure more or less accurate information about the haunts of ravens, which usually frequent only the loneliest and most inaccessible parts of the mountains.

The trail led through deep forests and up and across mountains, and was so covered with ice and snow as to be difficult going. At one point, the Collector showed me a place where he had been walking years ago, when he suddenly became conscious that he was being followed by something, or somebody. At a point where the trail doubled on itself, he ran back swiftly and silently, just in time to see a bay lynx—which had been trailing him, as those big cats sometimes will—dive into a nearby thicket. Anon he cheered the way with snake stories, for Seven Mountains in summer swarm with rattlesnakes and copperheads.

By the time he had finished it was dark, and I thought with a great longing of food and fire—especially fire. It did not seem possible to be so cold and still live. In the very nick of time, for me at least, we caught sight of the lamplight streaming from the windows of the Squire's house. Dripping, chilled, tired, and starving, we burst into Mrs. McMahon's immaculate kitchen and were treated by the old couple like a pair of long-lost sons. In less than two minutes, our waterlogged shoes were off, our wet coats and sogged sweaters spread out to dry, and we sat huddled over a glowing stove while Mrs. McMahon fried fish, made griddle cakes, and brewed hot tea simultaneously and with a swiftness that just saved two lives. We ate and ate and ate and ate, and then, in a huge feather bed, we slept and slept and slept and slept. Long after I have forgotten the difference between a tort and a contract and whether A. Edward Newton or Marie Corelli wrote the "Amenities," that dinner and that sleep will stand out in my memory.

The next morning, we started off again in a driving snowstorm to look at another nest some ten miles farther on. The first bird we met was a prairie horned lark flying over the valley, with its curious tossing, mounting flight, like a bunch of thistledown. It differs from the more common horned, or shore, lark by having a white instead of a yellow throat and eye line; and it nests in the mountain meadows in upper Pennsylvania, while its larger brother breeds in the far north.

Noon found us at a deer camp. Through the uncurtained windows we could see the mounted body of a golden eagle, which, after stalking and destroying one by one a whole flock of wild turkeys, had come to an ignoble end while gorged on the carcass of a dead deer. The man who captured it by throwing his coat over its head thought at first that it was a turkey buzzard, which southern bird, curiously enough, finds its way through the valleys up into these northern mountains. In fact, the Collector once found a buzzard's nest just across a ravine from the nest of a raven. Beyond the camp, on the other side of a rushing torrent, we found another raven's nest swaying in the gale, in the very top of a slender forty-foot white pine, the only raven's nest the Collector had ever found in a tree. It was deserted, and we reached home late that night with frost bitten faces and ears, and without a sight of the eggs of the northern raven.

The next day we took a train, and traveled forty miles down the river to where, on a cliff overhanging the water, a pair of ravens had nested for the last fifty years. There we found numerous old nests, but never a trace of any that were fresh. There too we found a magnificent wild turkey hanging dead in a little apple tree; it had come to a miserable end by catching the toes of one foot in between two twigs in such a way that it could not release itself. The bright red color of its legs distinguished it from a tame turkey. The Collector confided to me that the ambition of his life was to find the nest of a wild turkey, which is the rarest of all Pennsylvania nests. Next to it, from a collecting standpoint, come the nests of the Northern raven, pileated woodpecker, and Blackburnian warbler, in the order named.

March 12, 1919, found me again on a raven hunt with the Collector. Before sunrise, I was dropped from a sleeper at a little mountain station set in a hill country full of broad fields, swift streams, and leafless trees, flanked by dark belts of pines and hemlocks. Beyond the hills was raven land, lonely, wind-swept, full of lavender and misty-purple mountains, with now and then a gap showing in their ramparts. It was in these gaps that the ravens nested, always on the north side, farthest from the sun. Nearby was Treaster's Valley, which old Dan Treaster won from a pack of black wolves before the Revolution. When he lay a-dying, three quarters of a century later, the wailing howl of a wolf pack sounded outside his cabin, although wolves had been gone from the Valley for fifty years. Old Dan sat up with the death sweat on his forehead and grinned. "They've come to see me off," he whispered and fell back dead.

They bred hunters in that Valley. Peter Penz, the Indian fighter, who celebrated his ninetieth birthday by killing a red bear, came from there. So did Jacob Quiggle, who killed a maned panther one winter night, under the light of a wind-swept moon, with his famous gun, Black Sam. Over on Panther's Run, not ten miles away, lived Solomon Miller, who shot the last wood bison, and died at the age of eighty-eight, clapping his hands and shouting the chorus of a hunting song.

As the light began to show in the eastern sky, came the first bird notes of the day. The caw of a crow, a snatch of song sparrow melody, the chirp of a robin, the fluted alto note of a blue bird, and the squeal of a red-tailed hawk sounded before the sun came up.

A change of trains, and I met the Collector, as enthusiastic as ever. Already that year he had found six ravens' nests with eggs in them, but the one he had promised to show me was the best of the lot. It was located in Poe's Gap, where local tradition hath it that the poet wooed, not unsuccessfully, a mountain girl, and wrote "The Raven" in her cabin. On the way to the Gap we heard and saw nineteen different kinds of birds, including siskin, fox sparrows, and killdeer, and saw a buzzard sail on black-fringed wings over the peaks. On a farmer's barn we saw a goshawk nailed, its blue-gray back and finely penciled breast unmistakable, even after the winter storms.

As we entered the Gap, patches of snow showed here and there, and a mad mountain brook of foaming gray water came frothing and raging to meet us. When we were full two hundred and fifty yards away from the nest, the female raven flapped and soared away. The nest itself was only thirty feet from the ground, on a shelf protected by a protruding ledge, some ten feet down from the top of the cliffs. Rigging a rope to a tree, I managed to swarm up and look at last on the eggs of a Northern raven. They were three in number, a full clutch. The number ranges from three to five, very rarely six, with one instance of seven. The eggs themselves were half as large again as those of a crow, and all different in coloration. One was light blue, flecked and speckled with brown and lavender; another heavily marked with lavender and greenish-brown; while the last was of a solid greenish-brown color.

The nest itself faced the Gap, and from it one could look clear across the forest to the settled country beyond, while behind the cliff stretched a range of low, unexplored mountains. The nest itself was made of smaller sticks than the one I had seen over at Seven Mountains, and had a double lining of brown and white deer hair, a fresh lining having been laid over that of the year before. As we climbed to the nest, the ravens soared near, giving only the hoarse "Crrruck." They have also a soft love note, which cannot be heard fifty yards away, and sounds something like the syllables "Ga-gl-gl-gli." As they soared near us, their plumage shone like black glass, and we could see the long tapered feathers of the neck swell whenever either of them croaked. They had a peculiar trick of gliding side by side and suddenly touching wings, overlapping each other for an instant. While we watched them, a red-shouldered hawk unwarily approached the Gap. In an instant, the male raven was upon him, and there was a sharp fight. The Buteo was not to be driven away easily, and made brave play with beak and talons; but he never had a chance. The raven glided round and round him with wonderful speed and smoothness, driving in blow after blow with his heavy, punishing beak, until the hawk was glad to escape.

For long and long I watched the dark, wise, mysterious birds circle through the blue sky. As I sat in their eyrie, I could look far, far across the forests and the ranges of hills, to where the ploughed fields began. Perhaps that poet whose heart strings were a lute, had looked from that same raven cliff before he went back to die among the tame folk, and wished that he could stay in wild folk land where he belonged.

VI

HIDDEN TREASURE

It cost me an appendix to become a treasure hunter, but it was worth the price. I really had very little use for that appendix anyway, while my membership in the Order of Treasure Hunters has brought me in several million dollars' worth of health and happiness.

It all began when I was sent from a city hospital to an old farmhouse in the northwestern corner of Connecticut, with instructions to avoid all but the most ladylike kind of exercise. Accordingly one morning I found myself tottering feebly along a wood road that led over Pond Hill, highly resolved to walk to Hen's Pine and back. This was the lone tree which stood on the crest of the wooded hill which, half a century ago, old Hen, a freed slave, had begged from the charcoal burners when they coaled that region. Hen's old horse,

Bill, is buried at its foot, and Hen had hoped to lie there himself with his axe, his fiddle, and his whip. Instead, he sleeps in a little graveyard on a bare hill beside his old master.

My path had just crossed a round green circle in the woods where an old charcoal pit had set its seal forever. Suddenly a brown bird flew up from beside the road a few yards ahead of me. If she had kept quiet, I never would have learned her secret. When, however, she came back, flying from branch to branch with fluttering wings and jerking tail, keeping up at the same time a rattle of alarm notes like a tiny machine gun, even a novice like myself would suspect a nest.

Fortunately a broken hazel bush marked the exact spot from which she had flown. On going there, and looking carefully near its base, I found what has always seemed to me one of the most beautifully hidden nests of all the hundreds which I have seen since—perhaps because it was my first rare nest. It was roofed in by the split hazel branch, and made of woven dry grass and leaves, with a scanty lining of horsehair and a flooring of leaf fragments. Inside were five eggs. Four of them were bluish-white, with aureoles of reddish-brown blotches around the blunt ends; but the fifth was larger, and was specked and splashed with blotches of rufous and brown-purple. Long afterwards I learned that this last egg was the fatal gift of that vampire the cowbird, and that by leaving it there I had doomed the four legitimate future birds of that nest to certain death. Sooner or later the deadly changeling would hatch from that egg and roll its foster brothers out of the nest to starve.

That day, however, I was ignorant even of the name of the bird whose nest I had found. For long I stood and gloated like a miser over the little jewel casket which the mother bird had shown me, and for the first time realized that anywhere in the woods and fields I might come upon other treasure hordes of the same kind. Then and there I became a treasure hunter. Ever since then I leave my treasures where I find them, so that my recollections of them may not be marred by any memories of fluttering, mourning mother birds. Aside from any sentimental reasons, it has always seemed to me that he who takes the eggs which he has discovered is guilty of the economic error of spending his principal. If left undisturbed, the nest will pay dividends in the way of information and observations which are worth more than the mere possession of the pierced and empty eggs.

All the time that I was studying this nest both the parent birds were moving around me in anxious circles. At times the mother bird would drop her wings and scurry along just in front of me, pretending that she was wounded nigh unto death and that, if I would but follow her away from the nest, she could easily be caught. Both the birds had brown backs and buff breasts and sides spotted with black, and constantly tilted their tails and walked instead of hopping. As soon as I came back to the farmhouse, I rummaged through colored charts and bird books until I had decided that the nest was that of a fox sparrow, which also has a brown back and a spotted breast. It was not until another year that I learned that the fox sparrow nests in the far North and that the bird whose home I had discovered was none other than the ovenbird—or golden-crowned accentor, to give him his more sonorous title. This is the bird which comes in late April or early May and sings all through the woods the best example of a crescendo song in all bird music. His nest on the ground usually has a domed overhanging roof which makes it resemble an old-fashioned Dutch oven.

In spite of my ignorance there followed the happiest week of my life. I forgot that I was an invalid, as well as all the injunctions of my doctor. From morning until night I hunted birds' nests. As usual, fortune favored the novice, and I found nests that first week which I have found but few times since.

The very next morning, on the other side of Pond Hill I turned a sudden corner of the path through the dim green silence, and stepped right into a breakfast party. Mrs. Ruffed Grouse, known in that part of the country as partridge, was breakfasting in the open path with at least a dozen little grouse—or is it greese. Although taken by surprise, neither she nor her children hesitated for the fraction of a second. Falling upon the ground, she rolled and flapped as if in the last agonies of death, whining like a puppy and dragging herself almost to my feet. I looked away from the covey for a minute, to watch the bird struggling and whining at my very feet. As I stretched my hand out toward her, she feebly flopped away, still apparently well within reach. I took a step or so after her, to see if she would really permit herself to be caught. Suddenly realizing that she was only decoying me away from her brood, I turned back. Although I had gone less than six feet, and the little birds had been huddled together close to me on the bare path, they had absolutely disappeared. It seemed impossible that in a few seconds they could have gained the shelter of the woods or could have found cover in the scanty grass and scattered leaves close at hand. Not one could I find although I searched and searched. When I turned back the mother grouse was gone also, although I could hear her whining through the bushes.

Years later, again at the edge of the woods, one day early in June, I came upon another mother grouse leading a covey of little chicks, evidently just hatched, in single file out from the woods into the open, probably to catch grasshoppers. She went through the same performance as the first one, but this time I selected the two nearest chicks, which stood directly in front of me, and resolved that nothing would make me take my eyes away from them. Even as I watched, they melted away into the grass. One I found lying motionless on its side under a big brown leaf, looking exactly like its covering. The other I never did find. At first the leaf-hidden partridge refused to move even when I touched it, until I picked it up. Then it gave a shrill peep almost like a little chicken. Instantly the poor mother bird rushed up to my very feet and dashed her wings frantically against my legs, jumping up from the ground and whining so piteously that, after I had stroked her fuzzy, soft little chick, I put it back on the ground without any further examination. At once it disappeared, and the mother bird, still whining, also sidled away into the woods.

I hid behind an apple tree and waited nearly half an hour. At last from the woods sounded a low "Cluck, cluck, cluck," and instantly nine little partridge chicks, one by one, started up from the most impossible hiding places. It was like watching a resurrection. Some came from under leaves, others out of clumps of grass, and two or three rose from the almost bare ground, where they had lain in perfect concealment. Falling into single file, they hurried like little ghosts into the thicket, and the last I heard of that little family was a few soft and very satisfied clucks from the hidden mother bird.

During that golden week of treasure hunting I found a number of common nests which, although everyday affairs to an experienced ornithologist, were then, as they are now, a source of never-ending interest. There was the robin's nest partly made of wool, which I found in a thorn bush in the sheep pasture, with its four long, sky-blue eggs. Over in the woods, just back of the deserted house where Nat Bunker, the Indian, used to weave wonderful baskets out of maiden-hair stems, I found the nest of a wood thrush in a witch hazel about seven feet from the ground, by the simple process of running my head against the bush while going through the thick undergrowth. This accident bunted the mother thrush off the nest; and pulling the bush down, I peered in and saw three light-blue eggs.

If I had taken these eggs, as some bird's-nesters do, I never should have had the experience of actually seeing a little wood thrush come into the world. It was the last morning of my stay, and I had been making my round of nests, examining each one and beginning the bird notes which I have kept up ever since. As I pulled the nest down and looked at the three eggs, I suddenly saw a tiny black speck appear out of the side of one. Then the shell cracked and split, and I realized that what I had seen was the beak of the little bird within. In a moment the crack spread, and finally, with a tremendous effort, one half of the blue shell slid off and there in front of me, snugly resting in the other half of the shell, was the naked baby thrush, its long neck curled down beside its round stomach. Raising its blind head, it pressed against the confining shell, while its whole bare body shook with the heartthrobs of a new life. I realized that before my eyes this bare, blind bird was passing from one world into another; and when the birth was finally accomplished and, free from the prisoning shell, the little thrush lay panting on the bottom of the soft nest, I turned away with a certain sense of uplift that I had watched a fellow creature win a battle for a higher life.

It was another wood thrush's nest that same week, in the deep of a thicket, that gave me still another experience. The nest was in a tiny bush much lower than I have ever found a wood thrush's nest since. When the mother thrush left the nest, she wasted no time in idle alarm notes, but, circling around the bush, flew straight for my face. I ducked, and she went over me, only to turn and come back; and if I had not guarded myself by striking at her with my hands, I have no manner of doubt that she would have struck me with her beak.

In only one other instance in many years of bird's nesting have I ever been actually attacked by a nesting bird. Once in the twilight I had found my first and last nest of a Kentucky warbler on the edge of a wood. Taking a short cut through the trees, I was instantly assailed by a pair of screech owls, which flew directly at my face, snapping their beaks and making little wailing notes. The light was so dim and their flight so swift, that I actually ran out into the open, fearing lest they might land with beak or claw on my eyes.

It was on the third day that I found in a whitethorn bush the little horsehair nest of the chipping sparrow. This last summer, in the depths of Northern Canada, while hunting for such rare nests as the bay-breasted, the yellow-palm and the Tennessee warblers, I found the same little horsehair home of the chipping sparrow. I thought with this my last, as I did with my first, that there are no eggs of American birds more beautiful than those little blue, brown-flecked eggs of the dear gentle little chippy.

That same day, on the edge of the thick woods near the schoolhouse, I found swinging from maple saplings, four and five feet from the ground, the beautiful little woven baskets, thatched on the outside with white birch bark and lined within with pine needles, of the red-eyed vireo, with the black line through and the white line above her red eye. In the vast, bare hardhack pasture on the slope of Pond Hill, I watched a field sparrow fly down under a hardhack bush with a bug in its beak. Hurrying there, I found on the ground, concealed by the bush, her little nest of woven grass, with four little field sparrows inside, whose gaping beaks kept both father and mother field sparrow busy all day to fill them. As the parent birds flitted around me, I could see plainly the pink beak which distinguishes the field sparrow from all others of its family. Beside the brook, among the cattails on the ground, I found the rough nest of the red-winged blackbird, with its four eggs scrawled with strange black hieroglyphics.

The fourth day was another treasure-trove day. Just at dawn, in a dew-drenched thicket of spirea, I found three nests not six feet apart. In one, root-lined and thatched with strips of grape-vine bark, glowed the four deep blue eggs of the cat bird. The next nest, singularly deep and made of dried grass, was owned by a black-blue indigo bunting who, in spite of his intense coloring, seemed content with three washed-out white eggs and a light-brown wife. On the last nest the bird was brooding, and showed the golden-crowned head and the chestnut band along the side which has given its name to the chestnut-sided warbler. The nest, a humble affair of grass and hair, sheltered four wonderful eggs, pink-white, spotted at the largest end with flecks of chocolate and lilac and umber. Back of the thickets tottered an old, old house. For fifty years it had been leased to the wild folk. As I looked at it, one of them flitted out of the cellar way, a gray bird whose name note was phœbe. Just within the doorway, on an oak beam, I found her new-finished nest of fresh, bright, green moss.

All that morning I followed orchid-haunted paths through dim aisles of high pine trees without finding a nest. When I gave up hunting for them, they appeared. Toward noon I had put together a pocket rod and was wading down the bed of a little brook, to catch a few trout for lunch. In a little pool at the foot of a laurel bush, I landed a plump jeweled fish. I cast again, and my hook caught a low hanging branch. I gave the bough a shake, and from the foot of the bush a pale brown bird stole out. A moment later I was looking at my first veery's nest. It seemed strange to meet face to face this dweller in the dark woods. Usually I had heard his weird harp notes from the cool green depths of the thicket, but with never a glimpse of the singer. Today he sat on a low branch within six feet, and I could plainly see the faintly marked breast and the white spot under the beak which are the field marks of the veery, or Wilson's thrush. Both birds flittered around me like ghosts, saying faintly, "Wheer! wheer! wheer!" The nest was built just off the ground and lined with brown leaves, and held four of the most vivid blue eggs owned by any of the bird folk. The eggs of the catbird are of a deeper blue, but the strange vivid brightness of the veery's eggs makes all other blue eggs look faded by contrast.

All too soon my glorious week of treasure hunting drew to a close. For the last day were reserved the best two of my bird adventures. During the morning I had followed a wood road which led through dark woods into a marsh, and then up a wooded slope. I sat down to rest, and suddenly saw a gray bird fly up into a tree, alight on a limb, and before my eyes suddenly disappear. Bringing my field glasses to bear, I discovered saddled on that limb a lichen-covered nest, which looked so exactly like the limb itself that, if the bird had not shown me her home, I would never by any chance have discovered it. It was a far climb for an invalid, but I felt that life was not worth living unless I could have a closer look at this strange nest which had flashed into sight right before my eyes. Gruntingly I clambered up the trunk, and for the first time looked into the beautiful nest of the wood pewee. It was lined with down and held four perfect eggs, pearly-white and flecked with heavy brown and black spots.

For a long time I sat perched aloft, rejoicing over every perfect detail of that nest and the eggs, and studying the gentle, silent, anxious parent birds, of a dark-brownish-gray with two white wing bars and whitish underparts. I went back to lunch feeling that my last day had been well spent. However, the best was yet to be. I realize from later experiences in bird's nesting that all this has an impossible sound, but I can only say that I am setting down the happenings of this week of treasure hunting exactly as they came, and as they appear in the battered canvas-bound notebook in which I scrawled my field notes that summer. The Wild Folk had evidently decided to celebrate my discovery of their world by granting me seven days of nest-finding rarely vouchsafed even to veteran ornithologists.

It was at twilight, and I stood the edge of an old orchard where grew a white oak tree. As I looked away across the valley, I heard a humming noise, and through the dimming light saw a tiny bird buzzing through the air just overhead. As I watched, she alighted on a long limb about ten feet from the ground, and even an ignoramus like myself could recognize the long curved beak of the hummingbird. This one had a white instead of a crimson throat, which, I was to learn, marked the female. For an instant the little bird perched on the limb just over my head, and then suddenly sidled toward what seemed a tiny knot, but was not. Lest I be betrayed into further puns unworthy the fair fame of a bird student, I hasten to add that I had found the nest of a ruby-throated hummingbird.

It was too dark that evening to examine it more closely, but by sunrise the next morning I was on the spot with a stepladder, and with more delight than I have ever had in a nest since, looked down into the tiny lichen-covered, cobweb-stitched, thistledown-lined nest of this smallest of all our birds. Within were two tiny white eggs. The opening of the nest was just about the size of a quarter of a dollar, and it did not seem possible that two little birds could later be brooded and fed and reared in such a tiny cradle. The nest itself was saddled on the limb, which was perhaps four inches in diameter. It was so placed that the bottom of the nest did not rest directly on the limb, but hung a little to one side, so that the future little birds would rest in the swing of a hammock rather than on the hard foundation of the branch itself. The nest was lashed to the limb with strand after strand of cobwebs carried and wound around and around, until the whole structure was firmly anchored by myriads of almost invisible but tough little ropes. Inside, it was lined with the soft yellowish-white fluffy fleece found inside milkweed pods. Next came a layer of reddish-brown seed husks, all bound and lashed together with a network of cobwebs. On the outside was a layer of dull ashy-green lichen-scales. Each minute separate fragment was fitted into a mosaic which covered the whole nest. Outside of everything was another almost invisible network of cobwebs, like the net of a balloon which holds the round globe within. There must have been hundreds of gossamer strands making up this network, all so fine that only by the closest examination could they be seen.

Every bird's nest is a miracle, but I don't know any that is such a marvel of industry and ingenuity and beauty as that of the ruby-throated bird. Later on, when Mrs. Hummingbird was through with her home, I collected it, and had an opportunity of seeing just what the building of that nest meant to her—for, sad to say, Mr. H. B. never moves a claw to help in home building. The labor of collecting the spiderwebs alone, to say nothing of the hundreds of lichen flecks and seed husks, would seem to be almost impossible. On the outside of the nest I counted over a hundred separate bits of lichen, and then undoubtedly overlooked many; while in the next layer of seed husks there were probably at least three times as many. Bit by bit, flake by flake, the little worker had gathered her material, and from it had spun, and woven and built a nest which was not only soft and secure for her little ones, but, when finished, was absolutely disguised. No prowler on the ground or pirate of the air could tell that nest from a lichen-covered knot, unless, as had been my fortune, the little mother herself showed it to them.

So endeth the tale of my first treasure hunting. If you are not one of us, don't let another summer go by without joining our Order. You will find a wealth of happiness which no thief can steal nor misfortune lose, and which, as the years go by, pays ever-increasing dividends of joyous memories.

VII

BIRD'S-NESTING

It is the best of all out-of-door sports bar none. The thrill of hidden treasure, the lure of adventure, the joy of escape from indoor days—all these are part of it. Try it of a May day, or before sunrise some June morning. I have a friend who leads a double life. During business hours, he is the president of a bank. Outside of them he is the most abandoned bird's-nester of my acquaintance. If his depositors could see their president going up the side of a perpendicular oak tree with climbing-irons to look at the dizzy home of a red-tail hawk, or picking his way across bottomless bogs in search of the bittern's nest, there would probably be a run on his bank.

I know a woman seventy-two years young, who took up bird's-nesting in order to help forget a great sorrow. While her contemporaries are dozing their lives away in caps and easy chairs, she is afield in all sorts of weather, and sees more birds and finds more nests in a year than the average woman meets in a lifetime. Incidentally, she gets more health and happiness out of life than any woman of her age whom I have ever met.

Another woman, in a little town in New Jersey, by the sudden death of her husband was left alone with but little money and no friends. Moreover, her doctor advised her that she had only a year at most to live. One day, she found the nest of a prairie warbler, that little jewel casket lined with fern wool. It held four eggs like pink-flecked pearls. The very next day she bought a bird book, forgot all about herself, and spent the happiest months of her life hunting nests. At the end of a year in the open, she notified her indignant physician that she had become too much interested in her hobby to confirm his diagnosis. Today she supports herself happily by writing about what she sees and hears among the wild folk.

The moral of all this is, go bird's-nesting. This past summer, practicing what I preach, I spent all my spare holidays in May, June, and July hunting rare nests. Let me say in preface that I collect only with a notebook and a camera. Personally, I prefer to have memories and notes and pictures of my bird's nests rather than cabinets full of pierced and empty eggs; for I believe that a human who visits his brethren of the air as their friend will find out more about them than he who follows them about like a weasel, only to rob their nests.

The first of my bird holidays was on May 20th. Four of us were to meet at Mount Pocono, the highest mountain in Pennsylvania, on a hunt for the rare nest of that tiny bird, the golden-crowned kinglet. Late that evening, we reached the camp near the top of the mountain, where we were to make our headquarters. Up there, the weather had harked back to March, and the water froze on the porch that night. We pooled our blankets and curled up together for warmth.

At one a.m. a whippoorwill began his loud night-song. He always sings as if he were wound up, and in a great hurry to finish his song before the mechanism runs down. Later, in the darkness, we heard the drumming like distant thunder of the ruffed grouse. One of our party claims that on this mountain the grouse always drum at four-thirty in the morning; and his stock as an accurate ornithologist went above par when we examined our watches and found that it was just half past four. As the darkness turned to the dusk of dawn, the first day song was the beautiful minor strain of the white-throated sparrow. "O Canada, Canada, Canada," he fluted. Then came a snatch of the wheezing strain of the song sparrow. Finally, sweetest of all, sounded two or three tantalizing notes of the hermit thrush, pure, single, prolonged notes of wonderful sweetness, followed by two arpeggio chords.

We were up and out before sunrise; for he who would find rare nests must look for them while the birds are laying or brooding. Four hours distant, back in Philadelphia, summer had come. Here the trees showed the green tracery of early spring, and the apple trees were still in blossom, while everywhere the woods were white with the long pure snow petals of the shadblow. Someday, we four are going to follow Spring north, bird's-nesting all the way, until within the Arctic Circle we find her in mid-July.

Today, the first nest discovered was that of the junco, or slate-colored snowbird, whose jingling little song and the flutter of whose white skirts were everywhere throughout the woods. This one was close to the camp, hollowed out of the side of a bank of pine needles, and held four white eggs sparsely spotted with reddish-brown. The little mother bird chipped frantically, with a clicking note, which the Architect said always made him think that she carried pebbles in her throat.

There were trillions of trilliums, as the Artist remarked epigrammatically. Some were the common trilliums, of a dark garnet-red. Besides these, we found many of the rarer painted trilliums—a pure white triangle with a stained crimson reversed triangle in the centre. All of the trilliums are studies in triangles. The painted trillium has the crimson triangle in the centre, set on the white triangle, made up of three petals which, in their turn, are fixed in a reversed triangle of green sepals, and the whole blossom is set in a still larger triangle made up of three green leaves. Everywhere the woods were full of purple-pink rhodora, the earliest of the azaleas. Its blossoms were silver flecked with deeper-colored spots.

The next nest found was, to me, the most eventful one of the day, although not an especially rare one on that mountain. The Architect was walking beside one of the strange hummocks, which are thought to have been formed by buried tree trunks in the path of some old-time cyclone. Suddenly, his eye was caught by the gleam of four sky-blue eggs shining like turquoises from a nest directly on the ground, lined neatly with red-brown pine needles and with dry dark green moss on the outside, the hallmark of the nest of the hermit thrush. In front of it was a cushion of partridge berry vines, with their green leaves and red berries, while blueberry fronds, covered with tender green leaves, arched over the nest, and sprays of ground pine sheltered its sides. It was a fitting home for the beautiful twilight singer. The eggs of a hermit thrush actually seem to gleam from the ground, unlike the mottled and speckled and clouded eggs of most ground-nesters.

As the sun came up, the whole mountainside rang with birdsongs. There was the abrupt strain of the magnolia warbler, who to my ears says, "Wheedle, wheedle, whee-chee." The black-and-white warbler sang like a tiny, creaking wheel, as he ran up and down tree trunks. Down in the meadows beyond the lake, the long-tailed brown thrasher said, "Hello, hello! Come over here, come over here. There he goes, there he goes. Whoa, whoa, ha-ha, ha-ha." If you do not believe my reading of his song, listen the next time one sings to you, and see if these are not his exact words. Overhead, we often heard the squeal of the red-shouldered hawk, sounding almost like the cry of the blue jay. Then there was the loud yet gentle warble of the purple finch; and once we saw a beautiful rose-red male and his gray-brown wife feeding each other on a limb like a pair of lovebirds.

Another song which was interesting to me, because almost new, was that of the solitary or blue headed vireo, who sang, "See, see me-e. See me, you! you!" His whole song is in couplets. The Artist said that my rendering was too imaginative, and that what the bird really said was "Che-wee—che-woo, che-wee—chu, chu," which perhaps is more accurate.

Through appalling swamps and tangled thickets of rhododendron we were led by the Banker, who had highly resolved not to return without a sight of the golden-crowned kinglet's nest. Once we came to a large spruce, in which had been cut, in the living wood, great square holes like those in bar posts. On one side we counted five, on another three, while on the opposite side were no less than ten, with a new one on the top, cut right into the solid heart wood. It was a feeding tree of the great pileated woodpecker of the North, a magnificent black and white bird with a scarlet crest, nearly the size of a crow. All that morning we searched in vain for the kinglet's nest. Only as we came back to the cabin at noon for lunch, were our hopes raised.

As we walked down the trail, not a hundred yards from the cabin entrance, in a spruce tree, the Banker spied a great hanging nest made of wool and lined with feathers, from the top of which flew the only golden-crowned kinglet which we saw that day, with the orange patch on the top of his tiny head edged with black and yellow. The nest was empty, but the Banker felt that he had made the great discovery of his life, and discoursed learnedly on the industry of this tiny bird, which could find and carry such a mass of wool and build a nest at least a hundred times larger than itself. It was not until a month later that he was reluctantly convinced that what he had found was the nest of a deer mouse.

That afternoon, we skirted the little lake and saw, not forty feet above us, a bald eagle flying down toward us with its snowy neck and pure white tail. He flew with four or five quick flaps, and then would soar. In the distance, we saw another eagle pursued by a scurrilous cawing crow. The eagle flew over to the shore, and alighted and drank, and then, standing on the edge of the water, seemed to be fishing. His pursuer also alighted just behind him, and walked close up. Every time the eagle would turn, the crow would scuttle off, like some little blackguard boy following and reviling one of his elders. Several times, the crow flew over the head of the eagle and tried to gain courage enough to make a dab at him. Through it all, the king of birds paid absolutely no attention to his tormentor. The comparison of the crow with the eagle gave some idea of the size of the latter. He seemed over three times as large as the crow.

It was the Banker again, on the other side of the lake, who made the next discovery. We were hunting a little apart through the woods, when he announced from where he stood that he had just caught a glimpse of a Brewster's warbler. For the benefit of other bird students who are in my class, let me write what I learned that day in regard to said bird. A Brewster's warbler is the rare hybrid between the golden-winged warbler and the blue-winged warbler, more closely resembling the golden-winged. When it takes after the blue-winged, it is called the Lawrence warbler. This specimen we studied feather by feather for over half an hour at short range, and the experts of the party pronounced it beyond per-adventure a Brewster's warbler,—a bird not seen often in a lifetime. It was solid blue on the back, pearly white underneath, and showed white tail feathers, together with a greenish-yellow patch on the very crown of its head. It had two broad yellow wing bars, one large and the other small, and its white throat, innocent of any black mark, was the field mark by which it could be told from either of its parents or from its half-brother the Lawrence.

It was the Artist who made the last discovery of the day. Near the crest of the mountain, he gave a piercing cry and announced that he had discovered an Indian cobra. We all hastened to his rescue, and saw a fearsome sight. Coiled in front of him, hissed and struck a bloated, swollen snake, with a flattened head and up-turned snout. It was none other than the American puff adder, which ought to be called the bluff adder since, in spite of its threats, it is never known to bite, and is really a harmless and gentle snake.

The last thing the writer can remember of that trip was hearing, as he fell asleep, the Architect tell the Banker of the time he found two loon eggs, which a man had discovered on the top of a muskrat's house and put under one of his hens to hatch.

The next day we were back in Philadelphia and summer again, with a list of seventy-six different kinds of birds identified on the trip, and a total of ten nests found.

A few days later I went bird's-nesting with another friend in the very heart of the city of Camden. Through the manufacturing district, a sluggish creek winds its way past factory after factory. There, under a clump of golden-rod leaves, he showed me the nest of a spotted sandpiper, made of reeds lined with grass, containing four eggs—dark-brown eggs, spotted at the larger end with chocolate marks, and coming to a sharp point at the other end. Later on, I found another nest in the middle of a mass of horse tail. Then, in the very centre of a baseball diamond, not far from second base, on the naked ground, he showed me a killdeer's nest—a hollow scraped in the gravel, with four eggs which so matched the stones that they had escaped the notice of the players all around them. On the bank of the creek we found song sparrows' nests, and out in a patch of marsh on the very last tussock, the dried grass nest of a swamp sparrow, which was much thicker than the song sparrow's, while the four eggs were of a marbled warm brown and white.

Then we pushed on, still in the city limits, until we came to an old quarry bed half-filled with water, which had turned into a noisome bit of marshland. Pushing a rickety raft out through the muck and water reeds of the stagnant water, my friend showed me, on a clump of pickerel weed on a sunken stick, a nest of twigs on which was sitting a strange bird. Its long sharp beak pointed straight skyward. Its back was a combination of shades of soft reddish-browns, while its breast was reddish-brown streaked with white. The most curious things about it were its eyes. They were almost all pupil, with a bright golden ring around the extreme edge, and stared at us unwinkingly like a great snake. Although we came close up, the bird absolutely refused to leave her nest, and stabbed viciously at a stick, which I poked out toward her. Finally, not daring to trust my hand within reach of that stabbing yellow beak, I lifted her up bodily with the long stick, enough to show five whitish-blue eggs rounded at each end. It was the rare nest and eggs of the least bittern, a bird a little over a foot long, which has a strange habit of clutching with its claws the stalks of reeds and walking up them like a monkey. As we left, amid the clicking notes of the cricket frogs and the boom of the bull frogs, we heard a very low "Cluck, cluck, cluck." It was the least bittern singing the only song she knew, in celebration of the fact that she still had her eggs safe.

The Architect and myself decided to travel once again, later in the season, to the mountain, in the hope that we might make a better nesting record. We reached the cabin on June 17th, and again found ourselves back in spring. The peepers were still calling, and there were wild lilies-of-the-valley in the woods, and pink rose-hearted twin flowers, with their scent of heliotrope. Everywhere grew the dwarf cornel, or bunchberry, with its four white petals—the smallest of the dogwoods, which grows only a few inches high.

The first nest was found by me. It was built on a foundation of tiny twigs in a bush, and had a two story effect, the upper story being made of fine grass. As I came near the bush, a magnificent chestnut-sided warbler, with the bay patches on his sides and his yellow crown, made such an outcry that I suspected the nest and finally found it. There were three eggs in it and one tiny young bird, smaller than a bumblebee. Everywhere grew the beautiful northern azalea, of a clear pink with a perfume like sandalwood. The Canadian warbler, with its black necklace on its yellow breast, sang everywhere a song, which sounded like, "Ea-sy, ea-sy, you, you"; and we heard also the orange-throated Blackburnian warbler's wiry, thin notes.

Near the top of the mountain are two sphagnum bogs, difficult to find, but the home of many a rare bird. We finally located the larger of these bogs, and there the Artist made the great discovery of the day. Right out from underneath his foot, as he splashed through the wet moss, flew a yellowbellied flycatcher, which gives a note like the wood-pewee and whose nest had been found only once before in the state of Pennsylvania. Right in front of him, hidden in the deep moss, was this long-sought nest. It was set deep in club moss and lined with white pine needles, and contained four pinkish white eggs with an aureole around the larger end, with light rufous markings. It was so overshadowed with wintergreen leaves and aronia and bunchberries that, even after the Artist had pointed out the place to me, it was with very great difficulty that I found it.

As we crossed the marsh, I heard the song of the olive-backed thrush, which sounds to me like a cross between the notes of the wood thrush and the strange harp chords of the veery or Wilson thrush. In another part of the bog sang the rare Nashville warbler, whose nest we have yet to find. Its song starts like the creak of the black-and-white warbler, and ends like a chipping sparrow. In a marsh beyond the sphagnum bog, I found the nest of a Maryland yellowthroat, set in a yellow viburnum shrub some six inches from the ground. This nest is usually on the ground. It was set just as a gem is set in a ring, the setting consisting of leaves, which come up into five or six points. Held by the points is a little cup of grass. The eggs were the most beautiful we saw that day—of a pinkish-white with a wreath of chestnut blotches around the larger end. On the farther side of the marsh, a white-throated sparrow flew out from in front of me; and after a long search I found its nest—a little moss-rimmed cup of gray-green, yellow grass, containing four eggs of a faint blue clouded with chestnut, which was massed in large blotches at the larger end. With the four eggs was a dumpy young cow bird, that fatal changeling which is the death of so many little birds. In this case we saved four prospective white-throated sparrows from being starved to death by their ugly foster brother. The white-throat is a dear, gentle, little bird. Even its alarm notes are soft, instead of being harsh and disagreeable like those of most other sparrows.

The next day, I found a song sparrow's nest and a catbird's nest, and then in the midst of dark, cool woods, where an icy brown trout brook ran through a mass of rhododendron, a thrush suddenly slipped away ahead of me out of a clump of rhododendron bushes. The light color of the bird, and the lighter spotted breast, marked it as a veery or Wilson thrush. On looking at the bush, I saw the nest, a rough one made of hemlock twigs matted together, and lined with pine needles with a basis of leaves. Inside were four small eggs of a heavenly blue. They are among the smallest of all of our pure blue eggs.

That same day, the Artist found a beautiful nest of a black-throated blue warbler, also set in a rhododendron bush. The nest was made of the light inner bark of the rhododendron, which was of a bright yellow. Inside, it was lined with black and tan rootlets so fine that they look almost like horsehair. These are the same rootlets which the magnolia warbler uses to line its nest, and up to the present time no ornithologist whom I have met has been able to identify them.

"Can you go to Maryland today on a bird trip?" telephoned the Banker.

"No," said I, "lawyers have to work for a living."

"There'll be blue-gray gnatcatchers and mocking-birds and Acadian flycatchers," he tried again.

"No," said I.

"I've found out where the prothonotary warbler lives," he said once more.

"No," said I.

"We may find its nest," he continued. "No one up here has seen one for years."

"No," said I firmly. "What time does the train start?"

Sunset found me somewhere in Maryland. I was squeezed into a buggy built for one, along with the Miller, at whose house we were intending to stop, and the Banker, who is constructed on flowing, generous lines. We drove creakingly through miles and miles of blossoming peach orchards. At the Miller's house we ate the worst supper that money could buy. The Miller's wife had evidently been born a bad cook, and by careful practice had become worse. It was over at last, and the Banker and I retired to a room under the rafters, which contained one window and a mountainous bed. The rest of the space was taken up by mosquitoes. I undressed, jumped into the bed, and sank out of sight. The Banker located me by my muffled cries for help, and pulled me to the surface just in time to save my life. Thereafter we molded a conical crater in that feather bed and carefully fitted ourselves in, leaving a large air hole at the top.

It was a hot night. The mosquitoes bit steadily, and the feather bed was like a furnace seven times heated. All night long, a whippoorwill called his name under our window over three million times. The Banker said he counted the notes. Finally, after hours and hours of agony, I fell into a troubled sleep and was instantly awakened by the Banker, who said it was time to get up. We breakfasted on what remained of the corpse of the supper of the night before, which we found on the table. A few moments later, I was morosely moving an alleged boat through the mists of the morass.

Without further alliteration, let me chronicle what paid for all the toil, hardships, and privations of the trip. It was the sight of a bird of burnished gold flashing through the curling mists. "Tweet, tweet, tweet," he called ringingly as he flew. The note reminded me somewhat of the loud song of the Kentucky warbler, and the Banker, of the note of the solitary sandpiper. Every now and then we caught tantalizing glimpses of this warbler, which never by any chance stands still, but flits here and there among the trees over the water. From the trees I constantly heard squeaking notes, apparently of young birds. They sounded everywhere, and I decided that the whole marsh must be full of nests. The Banker laughed at my ignorance and told me that this was the note of the blue-gray gnatcatchers—"like a mouse with a toothache," as Chapman describes it. With great difficulty, I caught a glimpse of the tiny bird here and there among the treetops, and saw the two long feathers of its tail, and had a glimpse of the gray and white of its plumage. Some weeks before, the Banker had found down there one of its rare and beautiful nests, like a large hummingbird's nest, lined with down and thatched on the outside with lichens, and fastened to a high bough.

That day, I found the first nest of the prothonotary warbler. This bird uses deserted woodpeckers' nests in dead trees set in marshes, so it was necessary to paddle around to every dead tree which showed a hole. I finally saw a little red birch stub sticking up in the corner of the marsh, and rowing over to it, noticed a small hole in its side. Picking away the bark, I made it larger and a piece of the fresh green moss, from which the nest of the prothonotary warbler is always built, showed itself. Imbedded in the moss was a vivid orange-yellow feather, which could belong to no other bird. The nest was just built and contained no eggs.

The Banker found the second nest, in a willow stub ten feet from the ground, in an old downy woodpecker's nest. He found it by seeing the male bird fly into the hole. Climbing up to the nest, he found that in it were four young birds. Perching on a limb, he sat about four feet from the nest while I was in the boat perhaps ten feet away. The cock bird flew up with a Mayfly, making a soft alarm note something like that made by a field sparrow, only gentler. He flew up close to where my friend sat, and hesitated for a long while. Finally, the hungry little birds inside gave a prolonged squeak, which probably meant, "Mayflies immediately!" This was too much for Mr. Prothonotary. With a farewell look at the Banker, he turned his back and dived into the nest, placing himself entirely at the mercy of this giant who was keeping guard over his home. Seven times he did this while we watched, bringing in two beetles, a small wasp, a fly, and three Mayflies. The hen bird would come up time and time again with a fly in her beak, but never could quite muster up courage enough to go into the nest, but absent-mindedly swallowing the fly herself, would go off.

We had a wonderful chance to study the coloring of this rare bird. The cock bird had a bright black eye, which showed vividly against his yellow cheek, as did his long black bill. His colors were gray, yellow, and olive. The underside of his tail was pure white, and he had a white edge to his wings, while the top of the wings were greenish-yellow. The whole head, throat, and breast were of an intense golden, almost orange yellow, and the wings were bluish-gray. The bird itself was just about the size of the common black-and-white warbler. The female was of the same coloring, only much paler.

After that came the tragedy of the day for me. An overhanging bough knocked off my glasses, and they sank in the black waters of the marsh and continued to sink, in spite of my frantic groping and diving for them. The rest of the day I realized how the blinded galley slaves felt who were chained to the oar in mediæval times. The Banker kindly described to me all the sixty-five different kinds of birds he saw in that marsh. As my vision was limited to a range of about two feet, I did not see many more birds personally. In spite of my blinded condition, I did discover, however, another prothonotary's nest. I had taken hold of a rotten willow stub while pushing the boat through a thicket. It broke in my hand, and there, in an exposed downy woodpecker's hole, was a newly made nest of green moss, with a few twigs and bark strips on top, but no eggs. The fourth and last nest was found by the Banker, again in a downy's hole. He saw something move and thought it was a mouse or chickadee. Finally, a long bill came out of the hole and then a head. It was a hen prothonotary building her nest. She had the hole already filled with moss, and was bringing in grass, and would whirl around and around inside, modeling the nest carefully. Within, she had lined it with grass, just as a chipping sparrow's nest is lined with hair.

This was the last nest of the day. The Banker suggested that we stay over another night, but I felt that home was the best place for a blind man. My last memory of the golden prothonotary was hearing him call, "Tweet, tweet, tweet" from the willows, as we started back to the mill.

The last of my nesting trips was on July 7th. The Artist, in some mysterious way, had learned the secret of Tern Island, one of the few places on the New Jersey coast where the Wilson tern still nests. In a rickety old powerboat—probably it was the first one ever built—we traveled haltingly through the most intricate channels imaginable, and finally reached an island hidden by shoals and salt marshes, but whose farther beach faced the ocean. There, in a space about four hundred by one hundred feet, we found seventy nests of tern, containing a hundred and sixty-five eggs. Most of the nests contained two eggs, some three, and one, four. The nests were merely hollows in the sand, lined with bits of pure white shell. The usual color of the eggs was a blue-green background, heavily blotched with chocolate blotches, although I found one egg of a light green, speckled all over with light red specks. In only one nest was there a young bird. The little chick lay flat in the burning sun, while overhead hung the mother tern, pearl-white with black-tipped wings, making a grinding, scolding note. The young tern was downy like a duckling, and had tiny red feet and a pink beak tipped with black. We put up a stake to mark the nest, and later in the day, when we came back to photograph it, we found that the little tern had crawled out, followed the shadow which the stick had made, and lay with its head in the scanty shade far away from the nest.

We met other rare waterfowl that blazing day. We saw the rare piping plover, whose nest I was afterwards to find in Upper Canada, black skimmers, with their strange slant-cut beaks, black tern, least tern, loons, black-bellied plover, and everywhere throughout the salt meadows enormous great blue herons.

This was the last trip of our quartette for the summer, and we are looking forward to many more springs and summers among the bird folk. Let me end as I began—go bird's-nesting. Escape into the open from these narrow indoor days, and learn the way to where the wild folk dwell. Seek their patterans and share their secrets. In their land you will find the help of the hills, and hope wide as the world, and strength and youth and health and happiness in full measure. Try it.

VIII

THE TREASURE HUNT

I have always been of a very treasurous disposition. Such terms as ingots, doubloons, and
pieces-of-eight all my life long have been to me
words of power. In spite of these tendencies, I cannot
say that up to date I have unearthed much treasure. To
be sure, there was that day when I found a shiny quarter
in the mud on my way to school. Instead of being the
outcropping of a lode of currency, it turned out, however,
to be only a sporadic, solitary, companionless coin. Even
so, it was no mean find. I remember that it brought
into my young life a full pound of peppermint lozenges
tastefully decorated in red ink, with mottos of simple
diction and exquisite sentiment. "Remember me," and "I
love but dare not tell," were two of them, while another
was a manly query unanswered across the years which

read, "How about a kiss?" Although this treasure trove gained me a fleeting popularity, yet, like all treasure, it was soon gone. A prosaic teacher confiscated the bulk of the hoard, and all I gained from it was the privilege of learning by heart a poem of the late Mr. Longfellow. To this day those beautiful lines,—

> Be still, sad heart, and cease repining,
> Behind the clouds is the sun still shining,—

cause in me a slight sensation of nausea.

It is probably due to these lawless traits that in my meridian years I now hold the position which I do. Five and a half days in the week I practise law. On Saturday and Sunday afternoons and all holidays, legal and illegal, I am the Captain of a Robber Band, with all the perquisites and perils which go with that high office. Without vaunting myself unduly, I may claim to have fairly deserved my position. Starting as a mere friar in the band of one Robin Hood, my abilities as an outlaw brought me rapidly to the front. Thereafter, when that band was reorganized, I was unanimously offered the position once held by that implacable character who knew the Sesame Secret and pursued a Mr. Baba so unsuccessfully, yet so unflinchingly. Flattered by this recognition of qualities of leadership unsuspected by an unthinking world, I accepted the responsibilities of the captaincy. They were shared by First-Lieutenant Trottie, Second-Lieutenant Honey, Sergeant Henny-Penny, and Corporal Alice-Palace. There were no privates.

It was on a spring evening soon after the aforesaid election that the Band met. The Captain spoke with the stern brevity which characterizes all great leaders.

"Comrades," he announced, shutting the door and looking carefully under the sofa to make sure that there were no spies about, "I have just heard that there is a treasure not many miles from here. All those in favor of a treasure hunt tomorrow will kindly make a loud noise."

The vote was probably the finest collection of assorted sounds ever heard outside of a shipyard. Right in the middle of it, the door burst open, and in rushed Minnie, the cook, with a dipper of water, under the impression that her favorite fear of fire had at last come to pass. Close behind her was the Quartermaster-General, sometimes known as Mother, while almost at the same instant old John, the gardener, ran up on the porch with an axe, shouting hopefully, "Hould him! I'm comin'!" under the impression that there was a fight of sorts well under way.

The voting stopped suddenly, and the Captain looked quite ashamed as he explained. Mother pretended to be very indignant.

"Someday," she said, "you'll all be in terrible danger and you'll shout and yell and scream and bellow for help but not one of us will come, will we, John?"

"Divil a step," called back John, as he clumped disappointedly down the steps, his unused axe over his shoulder.

The Quartermaster-General agreed to withdraw her threat only after the Captain had pledged the honor of the Band that there should be no further disgustful noises within the house. Thereafter there were hurryings and skurryings and dashings to and fro, in preparation for the great adventure. Honey put fresh rubbers on his trusty slingshot, with which he could frequently hit a barn door at five paces. Trottie oiled up the air rifle, which he was only allowed to use in windowless wildernesses. Henny-Penny kept up such a fusillade with his new popgun, that the Captain threatened to send him forth unarmed on the morrow if he heard but one more pop. Alice-Palace's practice, however, was the most spectacular. She had a water pistol which, when properly charged, would propel a stream of water an unbelievable distance. From the bathroom door she took a snap shot at Henny-Penny, who was approaching her confidingly. The charge took effect in the very center of a large pink ear, and it was a long time before Henny-Penny could be convinced that he was not mortally wounded.

At last the Captain ordered bed and perfect silence within fifteen minutes, under penalty of being shot at sunrise.

"Nobody couldn't shoot me at sunrise," boasted Corporal Alice-Palace, as she started up the stairs, " 'cause I wouldn't get up."

The next morning at dawn, from the Captain's room sounded the clear whistle of the cardinal grosbeak—the adventure call of the Band. Followed thumps, splashings, and the sounds of rapid dressing from the third story where the Band bivouacked.

"If there be any here," announced the Captain after breakfast, "who for the sake of their wives and families wish to draw back, now is the time. Once on the way, it will be too late."

"I haven't got any wife," piped up Henny-Penny, "nor any family 'cept this one, but I want to come."

Similar sentiments were expressed by the rest of the Band. The Captain said that it made the blood run faster in his shriveled old veins to have such gallant comrades.

Purple grackles creaked and clattered in the trees, and the bushes were full of song-sparrow notes, as the Band hurried away from the house line toward the Land of the Wild Folk, where Romance still dwells and adventures lurk behind every bush. A tottering stone chimney marked its boundaries. There old Roberts Road began. On and beyond Roberts Road anything might happen.

Each one of the Band, in addition to the lethal weapons already set forth, carried a notebook and a pencil with which to keep a list of all birds seen and heard, with notes on the same. Even Corporal Alice-Palace, who was only six, carried a blank book about the size of a geography. To date it contained this single entry: "Robbins eat wormes. I saw him do it."

The Quartermaster-General, despite the difficulty of the evening before, had seen to it that the Band carried with them the very finest lunch that any treasure hunters ever had since Pizarro dined with the Inca of Peru.

As they moved deep and deeper into Wild Folk Land the air was full of birdsongs. The Captain made them stop and listen to the singing sparrows.

First there was the song sparrow, who begins with three notes and wheezes a little as he sings. It took them longer to learn the quieter song of the vesper sparrow, with the flash of white in his tail feathers. His song always starts with two dreamy, contralto notes and dies away in a spray of soprano twitterings. Then there were the silver flute notes of the little pink-beaked field sparrow, which they were to hear later across darkling meadows, and the strange minor strains of the white-throated sparrow.

Before long, a sudden thirst came upon Sergeant Henny-Penny. Fortunately they were near the bubbling spring that marked the beginning of Fox Valley, and the whole Band halted and drank in the most advanced military manner, to wit, by bending the rims of their felt hats into a cup. This method the Captain assured them was far superior to the more usual system of lying flat on their tummies, and had the approval of all great military leaders from Gideon down.

Right in the very midst of their drinking, there sounded from the thicket a hurried warble of a mellow timbre, the woodwind of the sparrow orchestra, and they caught a fleeting glimpse of the gray and tawny which is worn only by the fox sparrow, the largest of the sparrows and the sweetest and rarest singer of them all. A moment later a song sparrow sang. When he stopped, the strain was taken up by the fox sparrow in another key. Three times through he sang the twelve-note melody of the song sparrow, and his golden voice made the notes of the other sound pitifully thin and reedy. Then the fox sparrow threw in for good measure a few extemporaneous whistled strains of his own, and seemed to wait expectantly—but the song sparrow sang no more.

Through the long narrow valley, hidden between two green hills, marched the Band, following the hidden safe path that generations of foxes had made through the very middle of a treacherous marsh. As the road bent in toward Darby Creek, there sounded the watchman's rattle of the first kingfisher they had heard that year; and as they came to the creek itself, a vast blue-gray bird with a long neck and bill flapped up ahead of them. It was so enormous that Alice-Palace was positive that it was a roc; but it turned out to be the great blue heron, the largest bird in Eastern America.

From the marshy fields swept great flocks of red winged blackbirds, each one showing a yellow-bordered, crimson epaulet, proof positive that Mrs. Blackbird was still in the South. Mrs. Robin had come back the week before, which accounted for the joy songs which sounded from every treetop. Until she comes, the robin's song is faint and thin and infrequent. Beyond the creek they heard the "Quick, quick, quick," of the flicker calling to spring, and before long they came to the tree where he had hollowed his hole. A most intelligent flicker he was, too, for his shaft was sunk directly under a sign which read "No Shooting Here."

From behind them as they marched, tolled the low sweet bell notes of the mourning dove—"Ah—coo, coo, coo." The Captain tried to imitate the sound, and the harassed bird stood it as long as he could, but finally flew away with whistling wings. Then the Captain told the

Band of a brave mother dove whose nest he once found on the last day of March. It was only a flat platform of dry sticks in a spruce tree, and held two pearly-white eggs. The day after he found it, there came a sudden snowstorm, and when he saw the nest again, it was covered with snow—but there was the mother bird still brooding her dear-loved eggs, with her head just showing above the drifted whiteness.

Beside the ruins of a spring house, a gray bird with a tilting tail said, "Phœ, bee-bee, bee." It was the little phœbe, so glad to be back that he stuttered when he called his name. Thereafter the Captain was moved to relate another anecdote. It seemed a friend of his had stopped a pair of robins from nesting over a hammock hung under an apple tree, by nailing a stuffed cat right beside their bough. Whereupon the two robins, when they came the next morning, fled with loud chirps of dismay. When two phœbes started to build on his porch, he tried the same plan. He was called out of town the next day, and when he came back a week later he found that the phœbes had deserted their old nest. They had however built a new one—on top of the cat's head.

As the Band swung back into the far end of Roberts Road, the Captain's eye caught the gleam of a half-healed notch which he had cut in a pin oak sapling the year before, at the top of a high bank, to mark the winter quarters of a colony of blacksnakes. He halted the Band, and one by one they clambered up the slope, stopping puffingly at the first ledge, and searching the withered grass and gray rocks above for any black, sinister shapes. Suddenly Honey did a remarkable performance in the standing-back-broad-jump, finishing by rolling clear to the foot of the bank. Right where he had stood lay a hale and hearty specimen of a blacksnake nearly five feet long. Evidently it had only just awakened from its winter sleep, for there were clay smears on the smooth, satiny scales, and even a patch of clay between the golden, unwinking eyes. Only the flickering of a long, black, forked tongue showed that his snakeship was alive. Then it was that the Captain lived up to the requirements of his position by picking up that blacksnake with what he fondly believed to be an air of unconcern. He showed the awe-stricken Band that the pupil of the snake's eye was a circle, instead of the oval which is the hallmark of that fatal family of pit vipers to which the rattlesnake, copperhead, and moccasin belong.

"If you have any doubt about a snake," lectured the Captain, "pick it up and look it firmly in the eye. If the pupil is oval—drop it. Perhaps, however," he went on reflectively, "it would be better to get someone else to do the picking-up part."

When the Band learned from the Captain that it was the creditable custom of the Zoölogical Gardens to give free entry to such as bore with them as a gift a snake of size, their views toward the captive changed considerably. Said snake was now legal tender, to be cherished accordingly. It was the resourceful First Lieutenant Trottie who solved all difficulties in regard to transportation. He hurriedly removed a stocking, and the snake was inserted therein, giving the stocking that knobbed, lumpy appearance usually seen in such articles only at Christmas time.

From the Den, the Band marched to a bowl shaped meadow not far from old Tory Bridge, under which a Revolutionary soldier hid with his horse while his pursuers thundered overhead, well-nigh a century and a half ago. On three sides of the field the green turf sloped down to a long level stretch, covered by a thin growth of different trees, centering on a thicket through which trickled a little stream. Near the fence on a white oak tree some ill-tempered owner had fastened a fierce sign which read: "Keep out. Trespassers will be shot without notice." The cross owner had been gone many a long year, but the sign still stood, and it always gave the Band a delightful thrill to read it.

At the edge of the grove the Captain halted them all.

"Comrades," he said in a whisper, "I have heard rumors that there is a clue to the treasure hidden in the sign tree."

It was enough. With one accord the Band sprang upon that defenseless tree. Some searched among its gnarled roots. Others examined the lower branches. It was Henny-Penny, however, who boosted by Alice-Palace, fumbled back of the threatening old sign and drew out a crumpled slip of grimy paper. On it had been laboriously inscribed in some red fluid, presumably blood, a skull and crossbones. Underneath, in a very bad hand, was written: "By the roots of the nearest black-walnut tree. Captain Kidd."

There was a moment's check. It was Honey who recognized the tree by its crooked clutching twigs, and found at its roots a crumpled piece of paper which said: "Go to the nearest tulip tree. Blackbeard the Pirate." It was Trottie who remembered that a tulip tree has square leaves, and it was he who found the message which read: "I am buried under a stone which stands between a spicebush and a white-ash tree." They all knew the spicebush, with its brittle twigs and pungent bark which was made to be nibbled, and under the stone they found a note which said: "Look in the crotch of a dogwood tree. If you will listen you will hear its bark"; which made the Band laugh like anything.

The last message of all read: "I am swinging in a vireo's nest on the branch of a sour-gum tree." That was a puzzle which held the Band hunting like beagles in check for a long time. Corporal Alice-Palace at last spied the bleached little basket nest at the end of a low limb. Inside was a bit of paper which, when unfolded, seemed to be entirely blank. So were the face of the Band as they looked. It was the Captain again who saved the day.

"I have heard," he whispered, "that sometimes pirates write in lemon juice, which makes an invisible ink that needs heat to bring it out. Like the Gold-Bug, you know."

It was enough. In less than sixty seconds, sun time, the Band had built a tiny fire after the most approved Indian method, and as soon as it began to crackle, the paper was held as close to the blaze as possible. The Captain had the right idea. As the paper bent under the heat, on its white surface brown tracings appeared, which slowly formed letters and then words, until they could all read: "I am in the hidey-hole of the chimney of the Haunted House. The Treasure."

For a moment the Band stared at each other in silence. They had made a special study of pirates, black, white, yellow, and mixed. Haunted houses, however, were beyond their bailiwick. It spoke well for the iron discipline and high hearts of the company that not one of them faltered. Led by dauntless Sergeant Henny-Penny, they crossed the creek in single file on a tippy tree trunk. Half hidden in the bushes above, a gaunt stone house stared down at them out of empty window sockets like a skull. Through the thicket and straight up the slope the Band charged, with such speed that the Captain was hard put to keep up with his gallant officers. They never halted until they stood at the threshold of the House itself. Under the bowed lintel the Band marched, and never halted until they reached the vast fireplace which took in a whole side of the room. The floorings of the House had gone, and nothing but the naked beams remained, save for a patch of warped boards far up against the stone chimney where the attic used to be. It was plainly there that they must look for the hidey-hole.

The Captain showed his followers how in one of the window ledges the broken ends of the joists made a rude ladder. Up this the Band clambered to the first tier of joists, without any mishap save that the Captain's hat fell off and landed in front of the fireplace.

As they all roosted like chickens on the beams, there sounded a footstep just outside. The Band stood stony still and held their breath. Through the dim doorway came the furtive figure of a man. In one hand he carried a basket, while the other was clinched on a butcher knife well fitted for dark and desperate deeds. Although the basket seemed to be filled with dandelion greens, no one could tell what dreadful, dripping secret might be concealed underneath. For a minute the stranger looked uneasily around the shadowy room, and when his eye caught sight of the Captain's hat, he started back and peered into every corner, while the Band stood taut and tense just over his unsuspecting head. At last, however, evidently convinced that the hat was ownerless and abandoned, he picked it up and, taking off his own battered, shapeless head covering, started to try on the Captain's cherished felt. Then it was that the latter acted. Bending noiselessly down until his head was hardly a foot above the unwary wanderer's ear, he shouted in a deep, fierce, growly voice which the Band had never suspected him of having: —

"Drop that hat! Run for your life!"

The stranger obeyed both of these commands to the letter. Throwing away the hat as if it were red hot, he dashed out of the doorway and sprinted down the slope, scattering dandelion greens at every jump, and disappeared in the thicket beyond. Although the Captain laughed and laughed until he nearly fell off his beam, the rest of the Band feared the worst.

"He looked exactly like Black Dog," murmured Honey in a low voice.

"Yes," chimed in Trottie, "kind of slinky and tallowy."

Whereupon, in spite of the Captain's reassuring words, they made haste to find the Treasure, fearing lest at any moment they might hear the shrill and dreadful whistle which sounded on the night when Billy Bones died. Sidling along the beams in the wake of the Captain, they came to what remained of a crumbling staircase. One by one they passed up this until they reached the bit of attic flooring which they had seen from below. Sure enough, in one of the soft mica-schist rocks of the chimney, someone had chiseled a deep and delightful hidey-hole.

It was Lieutenant Trottie who, by virtue of his rank, first explored the unknown depths and drew therefrom a heavy, grimy canvas bag. When he undid the drawstring, a rolling mass of gold and silver nuggets rattled down on the dry boards, while the Band gasped at the sight of so much sudden wealth. A moment later a series of crunching noises showed that the treasure hunters had discovered that said gold and silver were only thin surface foils, each concealing a luscious heart of sweet chocolate. The Captain met their inquiring glances unmoved. "It only shows," he explained, "what thoughtful chaps pirates have become. They knew you couldn't use a bag of doubloons nowadays, but that sweet chocolate always comes in handy."

Hidden treasure is not a thing to be investigated scientifically, nor can anything restore a glamour once gone. Perhaps so unconsciously reasoned the Band as they followed the Captain down the steep stairs and the steeper ladder. Through the lilac bushes he led them around to the far side of the House. There the stairway had disappeared, and most of the sagging floor beams were broken. A limb of a nearby apple tree had thrust its way above the lilac thicket, until it nearly touched the ledge of a window half hidden by the boughs.

Up the apple tree the Captain clambered, followed by the Band, and walking out on the limb, led the way across the window ledge into a tiny room. For some unknown reason, amid the general wreckage and ruin of the House, this room still stood untouched and with its flooring unbroken. Even the walls, plastered a deep blue, showed scarcely a crack on their surface. Best of all, fronting the open dormer of the window, was a long, deep settee, with curly, carved legs and a bent, comfortable back. Its seat was so wide that the Corporal's legs stuck out straight in front of her when she sat down with the rest of the Band at the end of the line.

Framed in the broken sheathing and bleached stone of the window opening, there stretched out before them a vista of little valleys and round wooded hills, all feathery green with the new leaves of early spring. The Band felt that they occupied a strong and strategic position. A drop of some twenty feet sheer from the broken flooring behind them to the ground protected them against any rear attack, and the only entrance to their refuge was so shadowed and hidden by rose-red and snow-white apple blossoms that it would be a cunning and desperate foe indeed who could find or would storm their fastness.

With safety once secured, it was the unanimous feeling of the whole company that luncheon was the next and most pressing engagement for their consideration. An investigation of the commissary showed that the Quartermaster-General had merited promotion and decoration and citation and various other military honors, by reason of the unsurpassable quality of the rations for which she was responsible. When these were topped off by the Treasure for dessert, it was felt by the whole Band that this was a Day which thereafter would rank in their memories with Fourth of July and Thanksgiving, and press hard upon the heels even of Christmas Day itself.

After a rapturous half hour undisturbed by any desultory and unnecessary conversation, followed a chapter in the Adventures of Great-great Uncle Jake. Said relative had been a distant collateral connection of the Captain, and had fought through the Revolution, and, in the opinion of the Band, next to General Washington, had probably been most nearly responsible for the final success of the patriot arms. It was Uncle Jake who made General Putnam get off his horse into the mud and give the countersign. It was Uncle Jake who shot the Hessian who used to stand on an earthwork and make insulting gestures every morning toward the Continental camp. It was Uncle Jake again who, when he was captured, broke his way out of the Hulks, and swam ashore one stormy night. Today the Captain had bethought himself of a rather unusual experience which Uncle Jake once had while hunting bears.

"It was during a February thaw," he began. "Uncle Jake was coming down Pond Hill, when he stepped into a mushy place back of a patch of bushes, and sank in up to his waist. He felt something soft under his feet and stamped down hard. A second later," continued the Captain impressively, "he wished he hadn't. Something rose right up underneath him, and the next thing poor old Uncle Jake knew, he was astride a big black bear, going downhill like mad—riding bear back as it were. You see," went on the Captain hurriedly, "Uncle Jake had stepped into a bear hole and waked up a bear by stamping on his back. He was in a bad fix. He didn't want to stay on and he didn't dare to get off. So what do you suppose he did?"

"Rode him up a tree," hazarded Henny-Penny.

"No," said the Captain. "He stuck on until they got to level ground. Then Uncle Jake drew his hunting knife and stabbed the old bear dead right through his neck, and afterwards made an overcoat out of its skin."

The Band felt that they could bear nothing further in the story line after this anecdote, and the Treasure having gone the way of all treasures, the march back was begun. It was the Captain who, on this homeward trip, discovered another treasure. They were passing a marshy swale of land, where a little stream trickled through a tangle of trees. From out of the thicket came an unknown birdcall. "Pip, pip, pip," it sounded. As they peered among the bushes, on a low branch the Captain saw six strange birds, all gold and white and black, with thick, white bills. Never had the Band seen him so excited before. He told them that the strangers were none other than a company of the rare evening grosbeaks, which had come down from the far Northwest, which had never before been reported in that county, and which few bird students ever meet in a whole lifetime, although he had found a flock in New Jersey a few months before. For long the Band stood and watched them. They flew down on the ground and began feeding on cherry pits, cracking the stones in their great bills. At times they would fly up into a tree and sidle along the limbs like little parrots. The females had mottled black-and-white wings and gray backs and breasts, while the males had golden breasts and backs, with wings half velvet-black and half ivory-white.

For a long time they all watched the birds and made notes, until the dimming light warned them that it was time to be on their way. In the twilight the hylas called across the marshes, and from upland meadows scores of meadowlarks cried, "Swee-eet, swee-eet." Westering down the sky sank the crescent new moon, with blazing Jupiter in her train. As the Band climbed Violet Hill and swung into the long lane which ended in home, they heard the last and loveliest birdsong of that whole dear day. Through the gathering darkness came a sweet and dreamy croon, the love song of the little owl. Even as they listened, the distant door of the house opened and, framed in the lamplight, waiting for them, was Mother, the best treasure of all.

IX

ORCHID HUNTING

My path led down the side of the lonely Barrack, as the coffin-shaped hill had been named. There I had been exploring a little mountain stream, which I had fondly and mistakenly hoped might prove to be a trout brook. The winding wood road passed through dim aisles of whispering pine trees. At a steep place, a bent green stem stretched half across the path, and from it swayed a rose-red flower like a hollow seashell carved out of jacinth. For the first time, I looked down on the moccasin flower or pink lady slipper (*Cypripedium acaule*), the largest of our native orchids.

For a long time I hung over the flower. Its discovery was a great moment, one of those that stand out among the thirty-six odd million of minutes that go to make up a long life. For the first time, my eyes were opened to see what a lovely thing a flower could be. In the half-light I knelt on the soft pine needles and studied long the hollow purple-pink shell, veined with crimson, set between two other tapering petals of greenish-purple, while a sepal of the same color curved overhead. The whole flower swayed between two large curved, grooved leaves.

Leaving the path, I began to hunt for others under the great trees, and at last came upon a whole congregation nodding and swaying in long rows around the vast trunks of white pines, which were old trees when this country was born.

From that day, I became a hunter of orchids and a haunter of far away forests and lonely marshlands and unvisited hilltops and mountain sides. Wherever the lovely hid-folk dwell, there go I. They are strange flowers, these orchids. When first they were made out of sunshine, mist, and dew, every color was granted them save one. They may wear snow-white, rose-red, pearl and gold, green and white, purple and gold, ivory and rose, yellow, gold and brown, every shade of crimson and pink. Only the blues are denied them.

Since that first great day, I have found the moccasin flower in many places—on the top of bare hills and in the black lands of northern Canada, where, four feet under the peat, the ice never melts even in mid summer. Once, I saw it by a sphagnum bog where I was hunting for the almost unknown nest of the Tennessee warbler, amid clouds of black flies and mosquitoes that stung like fire. Again, on the tip-top of Mount Pocono in Pennsylvania, I had just found the long sought nest of a chestnut-sided warbler. Even as I admired the male bird, with his white cheeks and golden head and chestnut-streaked sides, and the four eggs like flecked pink pearls, my eye caught a sight which brought me to my knees regardless for a moment of nest, eggs, birds, and all. Among rose-hearted twin flowers and wild lilies of the valley and snowy dwarf cornels swung three moccasin flowers in a line. The outer ones, like the guard stars of great Altair, were light in color. Between them gleamed, like the Eagle Star itself, a flower of deepest rose, an unearthly crystalline color, like a rain-drenched jacinth.

Another time, at the crest of a rattlesnake den, I found two of these pink pearls of the woods swinging above the velvet-black coils of a black timber rattlesnake. I picked my way down the mountain side, with Beauty in one hand and Death in the other, as I romantically remarked to the unimpressed snake collector who was waiting for me with an open gunny sack.

Then there was the day in the depths of the pine barrens, where stunted, three-leaved pitch pines took the place of the towering, five-leaved white pine of the North. The woods looked like a shimmering pool of changing greens lapping over a white sand land that had been thrust up from the South into the very heart of the North. I followed a winding wood path along the high bank of a stream stained brown and steeped sweet with a million cedar roots. A mountain laurel showed like a beautiful ghost against the dark water—a glory of white, pink-flecked flowers.

Through dripping branches of withewood and star-leaved sweet gum saplings, the path twisted. Suddenly, at the very edge of the bank, out of a mass of hollow, crimson-streaked leaves filled with clear water, swung two glorious blossoms. Wine-red, aquamarine, pearl-white, and pale gold they gleamed and nodded from slender stems. It was the pitcher plant, which I had never seen in blossom before.

From the stream, the hidden path wound through thicket after thicket, sweet as spring, with the fragrance of the wild magnolia and the spicery of the gray-green bayberry. Its course was marked with white sand, part of the bed of some sea forgotten a hundred thousand years ago. By the side of the path showed the vivid crimson lake leaves of the wild ipecac, with its strange green flowers; while everywhere, as if set in snow, gleamed the green and gold of the Hudsonia, the barrens heather. The plants looked like tiny cedar trees laden down with thickly set blossoms of pure gold, which the wind spilled in little yellow drifts on the white sand. In the distance, through the trees, were glimpses of meadows, hazy purple with the blue toad flax. Beside the path showed here and there, the pale gold of the narrow-leaved sun-drops, with deep-orange stamens. Beyond were masses of lambskill, with its fatal leaves and crimson blossoms.

On and on the path led, past jade-green pools in which gleamed buds of the yellow pond lily, like lumps of floating gold. Among them were blossoms of the paler golden club, which looked like the tongue of a calla lily. At last, the path stretched straight toward the flat-topped mound that showed dim and fair through the low trees. The woods became still. Even the Maryland yellow-throat stopped singing, the prairie warbler no longer drawled his lazy notes, and the chewink, black and white and red all over, like the newspaper in the old conundrum, stopped calling his name from the thickets and singing, "Drink your tea!"

I knew that at last I had come upon a fairy hill, such a one wherein the shepherd heard a host of tiny voices singing a melody so haunting sweet that he always after remembered it, and which has since come down to us of today as the tune of Robin Adair. Listen as I would, however, there was no sound from the depths of this hill. Perhaps the sun was too high, for the fairy folk sing best in late twilight or early dawn.

The mound, like all fairy hills, was guarded. The path ran into a tangle of sand myrtle, with vivid little oval green leaves and feathery white, pink-centered blossoms. Just beyond stood a bush of poison sumac. Pushing aside the fierce branches, I went unscathed up the mound. At its very edge was another sentry. From under my feet sounded a deep, fierce hiss, and there across the path stretched the great body of a pine snake fully six feet long, all cream-white and umber-brown. Raising its strange pointed head, with its gold and black eyes, it hissed fearsomely. I had learned, however, that a pine snake's hiss is worse than its bite, and when I poked its rough, mottled body with my foot, it gave up pretending to be a dangerous snake and lazily moved off to some spot where it would not be disturbed by intruding humans.

The pyxies had carpeted the side of the mound thick with their wine-red and green moss, starred with hundreds of flat, five-petaled white blossoms. This celebrated pyxie moss is not a moss at all, but a tiny shrub. Near the summit of the mound the path was lost in a foam of the blue, lilac, and white butterfly blossoms of the lupine. Little clouds of fragrance drifted through the air, as the wind swayed rows and rows of the transparent bells of the leucothoe. Beyond the lupine stood a rank of dazzling white turkey beards, the xerophyllum of the botanists. The inmost circle of the mound was carpeted with dry gray reindeer moss, and before me, in the center of the circle, drooped on slender stems seven rose-red moccasin flowers.

> They have sought him high, they have sought him low,
>> They have sought him over down and lea;
> They have found him by the milk-white thorn
>> That guards the gates o' Faerie.

> 'T was bent beneath and blue above,
>> Their eyes were held that they might not see
> The kine that grazed beneath the knowes;
>> Oh, they were the Queens o' Faerie.

If only that day my eyes had been loosed like those of True Thomas, I too might have seen the fairy queens in all their regal beauty.

Wherever it be found, the moccasin flower will always hold me by its sheer beauty. Yet, to my memory,

none of them can approach the loveliness of that clois-
tered colony which I first found in the pinewood so
many years ago. Year after year I would visit them. Then
came a time when, for five years, I was not able to travel
to their home. When, at last, I made my pilgrimage
to where they grew, there was no cathedral of mighty
green arches roofed by a shimmering June sky; there
were no aisles of softly singing trees; and there were no
rows of sweet faces looking up at me and waiting for
my coming; only heaps of sawdust and hideous masses
of lopped branches showed where a steam sawmill had
cut its deadly way. Underneath the fallen dying boughs,
which had once waved above the world, companioned
only by sky and sun and the winds of heaven, I found
one last starveling blossom left of all her lovely company.
Protected no longer by the sheltering boughs, she was
bleached nearly white by the sun, and her stem crept
crookedly along the ground underneath the mass of
brush and litter which had once been a carpet of gold.
Never since that day have I visited the place where my
friends wait for me no more.

It was another orchid which, for eleven years on
the last day of every June, made me travel two hundred
miles due north. From an old farmhouse on the edge of
the Berkshires, I would start out in the dawn-dusk on
the first day of every July. The night hawks would still
be twanging above me as I followed, before sunrise, a
dim silent road over the hills all sweet with the scent of
wild grape and the drugged perfume of chestnut tassels.
At last, I would reach a barway sunken in masses of

sweetfern and shaded by thickets of alder and witch hazel.

There, a long forgotten wood road led to my Land of Heart's Desire. Parting the branches, I would step into the hush of the sleeping wood, pushing my way through masses of glossy, dark-green Christmas ferns and clumps of feathery, tossing maidenhair. Black-throated blue warblers sang above, and that ventriloquist, the ovenbird, would call from apparently a long way off, "Teacher, teacher, teacher," ending with a tremendous "TEACH!" right under my feet.

At last, there would loom up through the green tangle a squat broken white pine. That was my landmark. I would push my way through a tangle of sanicle, and beyond the trunk of a slim elm catch a gleam of white in the dusk. There, all rose-red and snow-white, with parted lips, waited for me the queen flower of the woods, the *Cypripedium reginæ*, the loveliest of all our orchids. Two narrow, white, beautiful curved petals stretched out at right angles, while above them towered a white sepal, the three together making a snowy cross. Below this cross hung the lip of the flower, a milk-white hollow shell fully an inch across and an inch deep, veined with crystalline pink which deepened into purple, growing more intense in color until the veins massed in a network of vivid violet just under the curved lips kissed by many a wandering wood bee. Inside the shell were spots of intense purple, showing through the transparent walls. The other two white sepals were joined together and hung as a single one behind the lip.

I had first found this orchid while hunting for a veery's nest in the marsh. At that time, nothing was showing except the leaves, which grow on tall, round, downy stems. They were beautifully curved at the margin, and were of a brilliant green, a little lighter on the under side than on the upper, and, at first sight, much like the leaves of the well-known marsh hellebore. That day was the beginning of a ten-year tryst, which I kept every summer with this wood queen. Then, alas, I lost her!

It came about thus. The marsh in which she hid was part of a thousand acres owned by a friend of mine, who was an enthusiastic and rival flower hunter. Each year, when I visited my colony of these queen orchids, I sent him one with my compliments and the assurance that the flower belonged to him because it was found on his land. I accompanied these gifts with various misleading messages as to where they grew. He would hunt and hunt, but find nothing but exasperation. Finally, he bribed me with an applewood corner cupboard I had long coveted, to show him the place. It was not fifty yards from the road, and when I took him to it he was overcome with emotion.

"I'll bet that I have tramped a hundred miles," he said plaintively, "through every spot on this farm except this one, looking for this flower. Nobody who knew anything about botany would ever think of looking here."

The next year, my wood lady did not meet me, nor the next, and I strongly suspect that she has been transplanted to some secret spot known to my unscrupulous botanical friend alone. Moreover, he has never yet paid me that corner cupboard.

I never saw the flower again, until last summer I visited a marsh in northern New Jersey, where I had been told by another orchid hunter that it grew. This marsh, I was warned, was a dangerous one. Cattle and men, too, in times past have perished in its depths. For eight unexplored miles, it stretched away in front of me. After many wanderings I at length found my way to Big Spring, a murky, malevolent pool set in dark woods, with the marsh stretching away beyond.

Not far away, in a limestone cliff, I came upon a deep burrow, in front of which was a sinister pile of picked bones of all sizes and shapes. The sight suggested delightful possibilities. Panthers, wolves, and ogres— anything might belong to such a pile of bones as that. I knew, however, that the last New Jersey wolf was killed a century or so ago. The burrow was undoubtedly too small for a panther, or even an undersized ogre. Accordingly, I was compelled reluctantly to assign the den to the more commonplace bay lynx, better known as the wildcat.

On these limestone rocks I found the curious walking fern, which loves limestone and no other. Both of the cliff brakes were there, too—the slender, with its dark, fragile, appealing beauty, and its hardier sister, the winter brake, whose leathery fronds are of a strange blue-green, a color not found in any other plant. Then there was the rattlesnake fern, a lover of deep and dank woods, with its golden-yellow seed cluster, or "rattle," growing from the centre of its fringed leaves. The oddest of all the ferns was the maidenhair spleenwort, whose tiny leaves are of the shape of those of the well-known maidenhair fern. When they are exposed to bright sunlight, all the fertile leaves, which have seeds on their surface, suddenly begin to move, and for three or four minutes vibrate back and forth as rapidly as the second hand of a watch.

Farther and farther I pushed on into the treacherous marsh, picking my way from tussock to tussock. Now and then, my foot would slip into black, quivering mire, thinly veiled by marsh grasses. When this happened, the whole swamp would shake and chuckle and lap at the skull-shaped tussocks and the bleached skeletons of drowned trees, which showed here and there. At last, when I had almost given up hope, I came upon a clump of the regal flowers growing, not in the swamp itself, but on a shaded bank sloping down from the encircling woods. Three of the plants had two flowers each, the rest only one. Among these was a single blossom, pure white without a trace of pink or purple. Although it was only the thirtieth of June, several of the flowers were already slightly withered and past their prime, showing that this orchid is at its best in New Jersey in the middle of June, rather than the end of the month, as in Connecticut. The perfect flowers were beautiful orchids, and had a rich fragrance, which I had never noticed in my Connecticut specimens. Yet, in some way, to me they lacked the charm and loveliness of my lost flowers of the North.

It was a cold May day. The Ornithologist and myself were climbing Kent Mountain, along with Jim Pan, the last of the Pequots. Whenever Jim drank too much hard cider, which was as often as he could get it, he would give terrible war whoops and tell how many palefaces his ancestors had scalped. He would usually end by threatening to do some free hand scalping on his own account—but he never did. He had a son named Tin Pan, who never talked unless he had something to say, which was not more than once or twice during the year.

The two lived all alone, in a little cabin on the slope of Kent Mountain. On the outside of Jim's door some wag once painted a skull and crossbones, one night when Jim was away on a hunt for some of the aforesaid hard cider. When the Last of the Pequots came back and saw what had been done, he swore mightily that he would leave said insignia there until he could wash them out with the heart's blood of the gifted artist. They still show faintly on the door, although Jim has slept for many a year in the little Indian cemetery on the mountain, beside his great-aunt Eunice who lived to be one hundred and four years old. Lest it may appear that Jim was an unduly fearsome Indian, let me hasten to add that there was never a kinder, happier, or more untruthful Pequot from the beginning to the end of that long-lost tribe.

On that day, the Ornithologist and myself were on our way to a rattlesnake den, the secret of which had been in the Pan family for some generations. In past years, Jim's forbears had done a thriving business in selling skins and rattlesnake oil, in the days when the rattlesnake shared with the skunk the honor of providing an unwilling cure for rheumatism. Our path led up through masses of color. There was the pale pure pink of the cranesbill or wild geranium, the yellow adder's tongue, and the faint blue-and-white porcelain petals of the hepatica, with cluster after cluster of the snowy, golden-hearted bloodroot whose frail blossoms last but for a day.

That very morning, a long delayed warbler-wave was breaking over the mountain, and the Ornithologist could hardly contain himself as he watched the different varieties pass by. I recall that we scored over twenty different kinds of warblers between dawn and dark, and I saw for the first time the Wilson's blackcap, with its bright yellow breast and tiny black crown, and the rare Cape May warbler, with its black-streaked yellow under parts and orange red cheeks. The richly dressed and sombre black-throated blue and bay-breasted were among the crowd, while black-throated greens, myrtles, magnolias, chestnut-sided, blackpolls, Canadians, red-starts, with their fan-shaped tails, and Blackburnians, with their flaming throats and breasts glowing like live coals, went by in a never-ending procession.

All the way, Jim kept up a steady flow of anecdote. I can remember only one, a blood-curdling story about a man from Bridgeport, name not given, who caught a rattlesnake while on a hunt with Jim, but who let go while attempting to put it into the bag, whereupon the rattlesnake bit him as it dropped.

"Did he die?" queried the writer and the Ornithologist in chorus.

"No, " said Jim proudly; "Tin and I saved his life."

"Whiskey?" ventured the writer.

"Not for snake bites," responded Jim simply.

"Well, how was it?" persisted the Ornithologist, hoping to learn of some mysterious Indian remedy.

"Well," said Jim, stretching out his tremendous arms like a great bear, "I held him tight and Tin here burned the place out. It took two matches and he yelled somethin' terrible. I told him we were savin' his life, but the fool said he would rather die of snakebite than be burned to death. You wouldn't suppose a grown man would make such a fuss over two little matches."

Finally, we reached the Den, a ledge of rocks near the top of the mountain, where for some unknown reason all the rattlesnakes for miles around were accustomed to hibernate during the winter and to remain for some weeks in the late spring before scattering through the valley. The Ornithologist and I fell unobtrusively to the rear, while the dauntless Pan led the van with a crotched stick. Suddenly Jim thrust one foot up into the air like a toe dancer, and pirouetted with amazing rapidity on the other. He had been in the very act of stepping over a small huckleberry bush, when he noted under its lee a rattlesnake in coil, about the size of a peck measure —as pretty a death trap as was ever set in the woods. By the time I got there, Jim had pinned the hissing heart-shaped head down with his forked stick, while the bloated, five-foot body was thrashing through the air in circles, the rattles whirring incessantly.

"Grab him just back of the stick," panted Jim, bearing down with all his weight, "and put him in the bag."

I paused.

"You're not scared, are you?" he inquired; while Tin, who had hurried up with a gunny sack, regarded me reproachfully.

"Certainly not," I assured him indignantly, "but I don't want to be selfish. Let Tin do it."

"No," said Jim firmly, "you're company. Tin can pick up rattlesnakes any day."

"Well, how about my friend?" I rejoined weakly.

The Ornithologist, who had been watching the scene from the far background, spoke up for himself.

"I wouldn't touch that damn snake," he said earnestly, "for eleven million dollars."

At this profanity the rattlesnake started another paroxysm of struggling, while his rattle sounded like an alarm clock. When he stopped to rest, the Ornithologist raised his price to an even billion—in gold. It was evident that I was the white man's hope. It would never do to let two members of a conquered race see a pale-face falter. Remembering Deerslayer at the stake, Daniel Boone, and sundry other brave white men without a cross, I set my teeth, gripped the rough, cold, scaly body just back of the crotched stick, and lifted. The great snake's black, fixed, devilish eyes looked into mine. If, in this world, there are peepholes into hell, they are found in the eyes of an enraged rattlesnake. As he came clear of the ground, he coiled round my arm to the elbow, so that the rattles sounded not a foot from my ear. Although the rattlesnake is not a constrictor, and there was no real danger, yet under the touch of his body my arm quivered like a tuning fork.

"What makes your arm shake so?" queried Jim, watching me critically.

"It's probably rheumatism," I assured him.

Suddenly, under my grip, the snake's mouth opened, showing on either side of the upper jaw ridges of white gum. From these suddenly flashed the movable fangs, which are always folded back until ready for use. They were hollow and of a glistening white. Halfway down on the side of each was a tiny hole, from which the yellow venom slowly oozed. I began tremulously to unwind my unwelcome armlet, while Tin waited with the open bag.

"Be sure you take your hand away quick after you drop him in," advised Jim.

"Don't you worry about that," I replied; "no man will ever get his hand away quicker than I'm going to."

Whereupon I unwound the rattling coils from my arm, and then broke all speed records in removing my hand from the neighborhood of that snake. This was my first introduction to the King of the Dark Places, the grim timber rattlesnake, the handsomest of all the thirteen varieties found within the United States.

On my way back from the den, it was Jim Pan who pointed out to me on the lower slope of the mountain the beautiful showy orchid (*Orchis spectabilis*). Between two oblong shining green leaves grew a loose spike of purple-pink and white butterfly blossoms. This is the first of the orchids to appear, and no more exquisite or beautiful flower could head the procession, which stretches from May until September. I find this flower but seldom, usually because I am not in the hill country early enough, although once I found a perfect flower in bloom as late as Decoration Day, a leftover from the first spring flowers.

It was Jim, too, that day, who quite appropriately showed me the rattlesnake plantain (*Goodyera pubescens*), with its rosette of green leaves heavily veined with white, from the centre of which in late summer grows a spike of crowded, greenish-white flowers. Under the doctrine of signatures, these leaves are still thought by many to be a sure cure for the bite of a rattlesnake. Personally, I would rather rely on a sharp knife and permanganate of potash. In the same group as the rattlesnake plantain are several varieties of lady's tresses, which grow in every damp meadow in midsummer and early fall. Little spikes of greenish-white flowers they are, growing out of what looks like a twisted or braided stem. Of them, all the most interesting to me is the grass-leaved lady's tresses (*Gyrostachys præcox*), where the flowers grow round and round the stem in a perfect spiral.

As I went on with my hunting, I learned that not all the members of the orchis family are beautiful. There is the coral root, with tiny dull brownish-purple flowers, which one finds growing in dry woods, often near colonies of the Indian pipe. The green and the ragged fringed orchids are other disappointing members. Yet, to a confirmed collector, even these poor relations of the family are full of interest. In fact, the second rarest orchid of our American list—the celebrated crane-fly orchid (*Tipularia unifolia*)—has a series of insignificant greenish-purple blossoms which look as much like mosquitoes or flies as anything else, and can be detected only with the greatest difficulty. Yet I am planning to take a journey of several hundred miles this very summer on the off-chance of seeing one of these flowers. Nearly as rare is the strange ram's head lady's-slipper (*Cypripedium arietinum*), the rarest of all the cypripedia and belonging to the same family as the glorious moccasin flower and queen flower. The lip of the ram's-head consists of a strange greenish pouch with purple streaks, shaped like the head of a ram.

There are scores of other odd, often lovely, and usually rare, members of the great orchis family, which can be met with from May to September. There is the beautiful golden whippoorwill's shoe, in two sizes (*Cypripedium hirsutum*, and *Cypripedium parviflorum*), and those lovely nymphs, rose-purple Arethusa (*Arethusa bulbosa*), and Calypso (*Calypso borealis*), with her purple blossom varied with pink and shading to yellow.

One of the fascinations of orchid hunting is the fact that you may suddenly light upon a strange orchid growing in a place which you have passed for years. Such a happening came to me the day when I first found the rose pogonia (*Pogonia ophioglossoides*). I was following a cow path through the hard hack pastures, which I had traveled perhaps a hundred times before. Suddenly, as I came to the slope of the upper pasture, growing in the wet bank of the deep cut trail, my eye caught sight of a little flower of the purest rose-pink, the color of the peach blossom, with a deeply fringed drooping lip, the whole flower springing from a slender stem with oval, grass-like leaves. To me, it had a fragrance like almonds, although others have found in it the scent of sweet violets or of fresh raspberries. It is the pogonia family which includes the rarest of all of our orchids, the almost unknown smaller whorled pogonia (*Pogonia affinis*). Few indeed have been the botanists who have seen even a pressed specimen of this strange flower.

Two weeks after I found the rose pogonia, I came again to visit her. To my astonishment and delight, by her side was growing another orchid, like some purple-pink butterfly, which had alighted on a long swaying stern. It was no other than the beautiful grass-pink (*Limodorum tuberosum*), which blooms in July, while the pogonia comes out in late June. The grass-pink has from two to six blossoms on each stem, and the yellow lip is above instead of below the flower, as in the case of most orchids. Years later, I was to find this orchid growing by scores in the pine barrens.

Last, but by no means least, is the great genus *Habenaria*—the exquisite fringed orchids. Purple, white, gold, and green—they wear all these colors. He who has never seen either the large or the small purple fringed orchid growing in the June or July meadows, or the flaming yellow fringed orchid all orange and gold in the August meadows, has still much for which to live.

It was with an orchid of this genus that I had my most recent adventure. I had traveled with the Botanist into the heart of the pine barrens. There may be places where more flowers and rarer flowers and sweeter flowers grow than in these barrens, but if so, the Botanist and I have never found the spot. From the early spring, when the water freezes in the hollow leaves of the pitcher plant, to the last gleam of the orange polygala in the late fall, we are always finding something rare and new. On that August day, we followed a dim path that led through thickets of scrub oak and sweet pepperbush. By its side grew clumps of deer grass, with its purple-pink petals and masses of orange-colored stamens. Sometimes, the path would disappear from sight in masses of hudsonia and sand-myrtle. Everywhere above the blueberry bushes flamed the regal Turk's-cap lily, with its curved fire-red petals. On high the stalks towered above a tangle of lesser plants bearing great candelabra of glorious blossoms.

Finally, we came to a little ditch, which some forgotten cranberry grower had dug through the barrens to a long deserted bog. On its side grew the rare threadleafed sundew, with its long thread-like leaf covered with tiny red hairs and speckled thick with glittering drops of dew; while here and there little insects, which had alighted on the sweet, fatal drops, were enmeshed in the entangling hairs. Well above the line of strangled insects on which it fed, a pink blossom smiled unconcernedly. Like the attractive lady mentioned in Proverbs, her house goes down into the chambers of death.

As we followed the dike, the air was sweet with the perfume of white alder. The long stream of brown cedar water was starred white with gleaming, fragrant water lilies. In a marsh by the ditch grew clumps of cotton grass or pussytoes, each stem of which bore a tuft of soft brown wool, like the down which a mother rabbit pulls from her breast when she lines her nest for her babies.

At last, we came to the abandoned cranberry bog. Suddenly, the Botanist jumped into the ditch, splashed his way across, and disappeared in the bog, waving his arms over his head. I found him on his knees in the wet sphagnum moss, chanting ecstatically the mystic word "Blephariglottis." In front of him, on a green stem, was clustered a mass of little flowers of incomparable whiteness, with fringed lips and long spikes. One petal bent like a canopy over the brown stamens, while the other two flared out on either side like the wings of tiny white butterflies. It was the white-fringed orchid (*Habenaria blephariglottis*). Beside her whiteness, even the snowy petals of the water lily and the white alder showed yellow tones. Like El Nath among the stars, the white-fringed orchid is the standard of whiteness for the flowers.

Three great blue herons flew over our heads, folded their wings, and alighted not thirty yards away—an unheard of proceeding for this wary bird. A Henslow sparrow sang his abrupt and, to us, almost unknown song. The Botanist neither saw nor heard. All the way home he was in a blissful daze, and when I said good-bye to him at the station, he only murmured happily "Blephariglottis."

X

THE MARSH DWELLERS

The sweet, hot, wild scent of the marsh came up to us. It was compounded of sun and wind and the clean dry smell of miles and miles of bleaching sedges, all mingled with the seethe and steam of a green blaze of growth that had leaped from the ooze to meet the summer. Through it all drifted tiny elusive puffs of fragrance from flowers hidden under thickets of willow and elderberry. The smooth petals of wild roses showed among the rushes, like coral set in jade. On the sides of burnt tussocks, where the new grass grew sparse as hair on a scarred skull, rue anemones trembled above their trefoil leaves. When the world was young they sprang from the tears which Aphrodite shed over the body of slain Adonis. Still the pale wind-driven flowers sway as if shaken by her sobs, and have the cold whiteness of him dead.

The leaves of the meadow rue, like some rare fern, showed here and there, but the clustered white flowers had not yet bloomed, nor the flat yellow blossoms of the shrubby cinquefoil. There were thickets of aronia or chokeberry, whose flat white blossoms and reddish bark showed its kinship to the apple tree. Among the pools gleamed marsh marigolds fresh from the mint of May, while deep down in the grass at the foot of the tussocks were white violets, short-stemmed and with the finest of umber-brown traceries at the centre of their petals. The blues and purples may or may not be sweet, but one can always count on the faint fragrance of the white.

We lay on the turf covering a ledge of smoky quartz thrust like a wedge into the marsh. Across a country of round green hills and fertile farms its squat bulk stretched unafraid, an untamed monster of another age. Beyond the long levels we could see Wolf Island, where a hunted wolf pack, protected by quagmires and trembling bogs, made its last stand two centuries ago. Where a fringe of trees showed the beginning of solid ground, a pair of hawks with long black-barred tails wheeled and screamed through the sky. "Geek, geek, geek, geek," they called, almost like a flicker, except that the tone was flatter. As they circled, both of them showed a snowy patch over the rump, the field mark of the marsh hawk. The male was a magnificent blue-gray bird, whose white underwings were tipped with black like those of a herring gull. We watched them delightedly, for the rare nest of the marsh hawk, the only one of our hawks which nests on the ground, was one of the possibilities of the marsh.

Suddenly we heard from behind us a sound that sent us crawling carefully up to the crest of the ridge. It was like the pouring of water out of some gigantic bottle or the gurgling suck of an old-fashioned pump: "Bloop—bloop, bloop, bloop, bloop"—it came to us with a strange subterranean timbre. The last time I had heard that note was in the pine barrens three years before. Then it sounded like the thudding of a mallet on a stake, for its quality always depends on the nature of the country across which it travels. From the top of our knoll we saw a rare sight. In the open pasture by the edge of the marsh stood a bird between two and three feet high, of a streaked brown color, with a black stripe down each side of its neck. Even as we watched, the bird began a series of extraordinary actions. Hunching its long neck far down between its shoulders, it suddenly thrust it up. As each section straightened, there came to us across the pasture the thudding, bubbling, watery note which we had first heard. It seemed impossible that a bird could make such a volume of sound. At times, after each "bloop," would come the sharp click of the bill as it rapidly opened and shut. Finally the singer convulsively straightened the last kink out of its neck and with a last retching note thrust its long yellow beak straight skyward. We had seen an American bittern boom—a rarer sight even than the drumming of a ruffed grouse or the strange flight song of the woodcock at twilight. Suddenly the bittern stopped and, hunching its neck, stepped stealthily, like a little old bent man, into the sedges. With its long beak pointing directly upward, it stood motionless and seemed to melt into the color of the withered rushes. One look away, and it was almost impossible for the eye to pick the bird out from its cover.

I turned to look at the marsh hawks just in time to see the female alight on the ground by a stunted willow bush far across the marsh. I waited, one, two, three minutes, but no bird rose. Evidently she was on the nest. Keeping my eye fixed on that special bush, which looked like a score of others, I plunged into the marsh, intending to bound like a chamois from crag to crag. On the second bound I slipped off a tussock and went up to my knees in mud and water. The rest of the way I ploughed along, making a noise at each step like the bittern's note. Halfway to the bush, the mother hawk rose and circled around us, screaming monotonously. For half an hour we searched back and forth without finding any nest. At last we hid in a willow thicket, thinking that perhaps the hawk might go back to her nest. Instead, both birds disappeared in some distant woods. The sun was getting low and we were miles from our inn; yet as this was the nearest either of us had ever been to finding a marsh hawk's nest, we decided to hunt on until dark.

I laid out a route from my bush to another about thirty yards away, and between those two as bounds planned to quarter back and forth over every square foot of ground, moving toward the woods where the hawks had gone. It seemed an almost hopeless hunt, for the marsh at this point was dry, with patches of bushes,

masses of sedge, and piled heaps here and there of dry
rushes. As I reached my farther boundary and was about
to return, I straightened my aching back and looked
beyond the bush. There, directly ahead, in a space fringed
by spirea bushes but in plain sight, lay a round nest on
the ground—about eight inches across and three inches
deep, made of coarse grasses ringed around with rushes.
Beneath the nest was a well-packed platform several
inches thick. I think that this was a natural pile of rushes
pressed down by the bird. There, under the open sky,
were five large eggs of a dirty bluish-white, nearly ready
to hatch. They were the size of a small hen's egg. The
very second I caught sight of the nest the mother hawk
came dashing through the air, from some unseen perch
where she had been watching me with her telescopic
eyes. Fifty feet away, she folded her wings and dived at
my head, falling through the air like a stone. With her
fierce unflinching eyes, half-open beak, and outspread
claws, she looked dangerous. Ten feet away, however,
she swooped up and circled off in ever-widening rings,
screaming mournfully. Beside the nest was one barred
tail feather.

> I crossed a moor, with a name of its own
>   And a certain use in the world no doubt,
> Yet a hand's breadth of it shines alone
>   'Mid the blank miles round about:
>
> For there I picked upon the heather
>   And there I put inside my breast

A moulted feather, an eagle feather!
Well, I forget the rest.

Something of this we felt as we lingered over this long-sought nest, making notes and photographs—our way of collecting.

Just at sunset we waded back and stopped at the little arm of the swamp where we had first heard the bittern. Suddenly from the sedges came a scolding little song that sounded like "Chop, chip-chop, chp'p'p'p," and we caught the merest glimpse of a tiny bird with a tip-tilted tail and brown back whose undersides seemed yellowish. It was none other than the rare short-billed marsh wren, next to the smallest of our Eastern birds, only the hummingbird being tinier. Neither of us had ever seen this marsh wren before, and we tramped back three long miles to town with a new bird, a new nest, and a new note to our credit in our out-of-doors account.

That night over a good dinner we were joined by the other two of our Four who for many happy years have hunted together. Just at dawn the next day, we all stole out of the sleeping inn and along the silent village streets, sweet with the scent of lilacs. Right in front of the town hall we found the first nest of the day. Cunningly hidden in the crotch of a sugar maple, just over the heads of hundreds of unseeing passersby, a robin had brooded day by day over four eggs whose heavenly blue made a jewel casket of her mud nest. I hope that the brave silent bird raised her babies and sent them out to add to the world's store of music and beauty.

Beyond the village we dragged a meadow. A long cord was tied to the ankles of two of us, and each walked away from the other until it was taut and then marched slowly through the fields. The moving line just swished the top of the long grass and flushed any ground birds that might be nesting within the area covered by the fifty-foot cord. Our first haul was a vesper sparrow's nest with one egg—the bird breaking cover near my end. Later in the day another of our party found a better nest of the same bird in the middle of a field, made and lined with grass and set in a little hollow in the ground. It held three eggs of a bluish white, blotched and clouded with umber and lavender at the larger ends. Two of the eggs were marked with black hieroglyphics like those seen in the eggs of an oriole or red-winged blackbird. The vesper is that gray sparrow which shows two white tail feathers when it flies, and sings an alto song whose first two notes are always in a different key from the rest of the strain.

In another field we flushed a bobolink. Unfortunately the Artist, whose duty it was to watch the rope, was at the moment gazing skywards at cloud effects, and though we burrowed and peered for a full hour in the fragrant dripping grass, we never found that nest. The home of a bobolink is one of the best hidden of all of our common ground builders. I remember one Decoration Day when I highly resolved to find a bobolink's nest in a field where several pairs were nesting. Early in my hunt I decided that the gay black-and-white males, which seemed to be flying and singing aimlessly, were really signaling my approach to the females on the nests. At any rate, the mother birds would rise far ahead as I came near, evidently after having run for long distances through the grass, and gave me no clue as to the whereabouts of their nests. I decided, however, that my only chance was to watch these females, knowing that an incubating bird will not leave her eggs for any great length of time. Accordingly, when the next streaked brown bird flew up far ahead of me, I settled down in the long grass with a field glass and carefully watched her flight. She crossed the meadow and alighted some three hundred yards away. In about fifteen minutes she came back and settled in the grass on a slope some distance from where she had flown out. Almost immediately she flew out again, probably warned by the male on guard. Once more she crossed the meadow, and this time stayed away so long that I nearly fell asleep in the drowsy, scented grass. In the meantime, one by one, the songs of the males, like the tinkling, gurgling notes of a trout brook, ceased, and my part of the meadow seemed deserted. Finally through my half-shut eyes I saw Mrs. Bobolink come flying low over the tops of the waving grass. As I lay perfectly still, she made a half circle around the slope and suddenly disappeared in the ripple of a green wave that rose to meet the wind. I marked the place by a tall weed stalk, and waited a minute to see whether this was another feint. As she did not appear, I ran up as rapidly and silently as possible before the father bird could spy me from the other side of the pasture and cry the alarm.

Perhaps he had become careless while rollicking with his friends. At any rate, when I reached the place there was no sign of any bobolink near me.

When I was a couple of yards away from the weed stalk, up sprang the female bobolink, apparently from almost the very spot I had noted. This was encouraging; it showed that she had not run through the grass any distance this time, either when flushed or when alighting. Almost immediately the truant father bird appeared and sang gayly near me, occasionally diving mysteriously and impressively into the grass in different places, as if visiting a nest. I was not to be distracted by any such tactics, but threw my hat to the exact spot from which, as I judged, the female had started. With this as a centre I pushed back the long grass and began to search the area of a five-foot circle, first looking hurriedly under the hat to make sure that it had not covered the nest. My search was all in vain, although it seemed to me that I examined every square inch of that circle. At last I decided that the sly birds had again deceived me. Taking up my hat, I was about to begin another watch, when, in the very spot where the hat had lain, I noticed that the long leaves of a narrow-leafed plantain at one place had been parted, showing a hole underneath. I carefully separated the leaves, and before me lay the long-desired nest. It was only a shallow hollow under the leaves, lined with fine dry grass and containing four dark eggs heavily blotched and marbled with red-brown.

It is probable that ordinarily, when the mother bird left the nest, she would arrange the leaves so as entirely to cover the hole beneath. If this were done, it would seem impossible that they concealed anything, for they would be apparently flat on the surface of the ground. My unexpected approach had flushed her before she had time to put back the leaves.

The pleasure of finding such a skillfully concealed nest is indescribable. The hunt is a contest between intelligence and instinct, where victory by no means always inclines to the human. As I looked down at the nest, I knew just how the talented recluse in "The Gold Bug" felt when, after solving the cryptogram and disposing of every difficulty, he at last gazed into the open treasure chest.

Today there was to be no such glorious experience, and we finally gave up the hunt and started back across the meadow. As we moved through the swishing grass, suddenly we heard a curious clicking bird note. "See-lick, see-lick, see-lick," it sounded, and we recognized the unfamiliar notes of that rare little black-striped sparrow, the Henslow. The last time we four had heard that note together was on a trip into the heart of the pine barrens, when we not only identified this bird for the first time, but also found its nest, a treasure trove indeed. Today we did not even get a glimpse of the bird.

Beyond the meadows we came face to face with the marsh itself, and plunged in to show the Banker and the Architect our marsh hawk's nest. On the way back the Artist made a discovery. Waist deep among the sedges, with the tiny marsh wrens chipping and bubbling all around him, he suddenly espied a round ball made of green grass fastened to the rushes with a little hole in one side.

"The nest of the short-billed marsh wren!" he declared loudly. We hurried to him. The nest was empty, but, as it was early for the wrens to be laying, this fact had no effect on his triumph. We admired the nest, the bird, and the discoverer freely—all except the Architect, who lingered behind the rest of us, regarding the nest with much suspicion. Suddenly he noted a movement in the grass, and as he watched, a tawny little meadow mouse climbed up the grass stems and popped into the hole in the side, to find out what this inquisitive race of giants had been doing to his house. It was pitiful to see the Artist. At first he denied the mouse. Then, when it dashed out in front of us, he claimed that its presence had nothing to do with the question of the ownership of the nest.

"Isn't it possible," he demanded bitterly, "that a well-behaved meadow mouse may make a neighborly call on a marsh wren?"

"No," replied the Architect decisively; and we started away from the discredited nest.

Later on, the Artist had his revenge. We were hunting everywhere for the bittern's nest. Suddenly, as the Artist stepped on a tussock, a large squawking bird flew out from under his foot. No wonder she squawked. He had stepped so nearly on top of her that, as she escaped, she left behind a handful of long, beautifully mottled tail feathers, unmistakably those of an English pheasant. The nest was at the side of the tussock, entirely covered over with the arched reeds, and contained fifteen eggs, three of which the clumsy foot of the Artist had broken. They were of a chocolate color and, curiously enough, almost identical in color and size with those of the American bittern, except that the inside of the shell of the broken eggs was a light blue. The nest itself was nearly eight inches across and about three inches deep, made entirely of grass. Hurriedly clearing away the broken eggs, we called the Architect from the far side of the marsh. He hastened up, took one look at the nest, and then told us solemnly that this was one of the most unusual occurrences known in ornithology. Three pairs of bitterns had joined housekeeping and laid eggs in the same nest. It was hard on the Architect that we should have flushed probably the only bird in the world whose eggs are almost identical in color and size with those of the American bittern, and it was not until the Artist produced the pheasant's tailfeathers that our friend would admit that there was anything wrong with his theory.

As we started to leave the place, I saw on the other side of the tussock the largest wood turtle I have ever met. Its legs and tail were of a bright brick-red, while the shell was beautifully carved in deep intaglios of dingy black and yellow. This turtle ranks next to the terrapin in taste, a fact which I proved the next day. As Mr. Wood Turtle is fond of bird's eggs, I strongly suspect that my capture of him was all that saved the lives of a round dozen of prospective pheasants. We had a leisurely lunch near one of the coldest bubbling springs in the world, seated on a high, dry ridge under the shade of a vast black-walnut tree. After lunch we crossed quaking, treacherous bogs, that lapped at our feet as we passed, and reached Wolf Island. It was made up of a series of rocky ridges, shaded with trees and masked by a dense undergrowth. Beneath the great boulders and at the base of tiny cliffs, we could trace dark holes and burrows where two centuries ago the celebrated pack made their home.

Beyond the Island a tawny bird slipped out of a tussock ahead of me, like a shadow. Hurrying to the place, I found the perfectly rounded nest of a veery thrush, lined with leaves and entirely arched over by the long marsh grass. From the brown leaf bed the four vivid blue eggs gleamed out of the green grass like turquoises set in malachite. The eggs of a catbird are of a deeper blue, and those of a hermit thrush of a purer tone, but of all the blue eggs, of robin, wood thrush, hermit thrush, bluebird, cuckoo, or catbird, there is none so vivid in its coloring as that of the veery. That nest with its beautiful setting stands out in my mind as a notable addition to my collection of out-of-door memories.

More searchings followed without results, until the sun was westering well down the sky. Five miles lay between us and clean clothes and a bath. Reluctantly we left the marsh, with our bittern's nest still unfound. As we approached the village, we saw showing over the meadows the edge of a continuation of the marsh, and decided that we had time for just one more exploring trip. Here we found the worst going of the day. In front of us were innumerable dry cattail stalks and hollow reed stems, while the mud was deeper and the mosquitoes were fiercer than in the main swamp.

At last the Banker and the Architect sat down exhausted under a tree, while the Artist and myself planned to cross to a fringe of woods on the farther side before giving up. In the middle of the marsh we separated, and before long I found myself on the trail of another marsh hawk's nest. It was evidently close at hand, for both the birds swooped down and circled around my head, calling frantically all the time. Look as I would, however, I could find no trace of the nest. We reached the woods without finding anything and came back together. When we were within two hundred yards of where the other two were luxuriously waiting for us in the shade, from under my very feet flapped a monstrous bird nearly three feet high. It was the bittern. I was so close that I could see the yellow bill, and the glossy black on the sides of the neck and tips of the wings, and the different shades of brown on back, head, and wings. As it sprang up, it gave a hoarse cry and flapped off with labored strokes of its broad wings. Right before me was a flat platform of reeds about a foot in diameter, well packed down and raised about five inches from the water. On this platform were a shred or so of down and four eggs of a dull coffee color. In a moment the Banker and the Architect were splashing and crackling through the mud and reeds, and we spent the last quarter-hour of our trip in admiring and photographing the much-desired nest.

So ended our visit to Wolf Island Marsh with a list of fifty-one birds seen and heard, and seven nests found, photographed, and enjoyed.

XI

THE SEVEN SLEEPERS

A thousand and a thousand years ago, seven saints hid from heathen persecutors among the cold mountains which circle Ephesus. The multitude who cried, "Great is Diana of the Ephesians!" are drifting dust, and the vast city itself but a mass of half buried ruins. Yet somewhere in a lonely cave sleep those seven holy men, unvexed by sorrow, untouched by time, until Christ comes again. So runs the legend.

It is a far cry to Ephesus, and whether the Seven still sleep there, who may say? Yet here and now seven other Sleepers live with us, who slumber through our winters, with hunger and cold and danger but a dream. Their names I once rhymed for some children of my acquaintance. As I am credibly advised that the progress of a camel through the eye of a needle is an easy process compared to having a poem printed by the Atlantic

Press, I hasten to include in this chapter the following exquisite bit of free verse (I call it free because I don't get anything extra for it).

> The Bat and the Bear, they never care
>   What winter winds may blow;
> The Jumping Mouse in his cozy house
>   Is safe from ice and snow.
> The Chipmunk and the Woodchuck,
>   The Skunk, who's slow but sure,
> The ringed Raccoon, who hates the moon,
>   Have found for cold the cure.

Something of the lives of these our brethren of the wild I have tried to set forth here—because I care for them all.

First comes the slyest, the shyest, and the stillest of the Seven—the black bear, who yet dwells among men when his old-time companions, the timber wolf and the panther, have been long gone. Silent as a shadow, he is with us far oftener than we know. Only a few years ago bears were found in New Jersey, in dense cedar swamps, unsuspected by a generation of nearby farmers. In Pennsylvania and New York they are increasing, and I have no doubt that they can still be found in parts of New England, from which they are supposed to have disappeared a half century ago. In fact, it is always unsafe to say that any of the wild folk have gone forever. I have lived to see a herd of seven Virginia deer feeding in my neighbor's cabbage patch in Connecticut, although neither my father nor my grandfather ever saw a wild deer in that state. In that same township, I once had a fleeting glimpse of an otter, and only last winter, within thirty miles of Philadelphia, I located a colony of beaver.

The black bear is nearly as black as a blacksnake, whose color is as perfect a standard of absolute black on earth as El Nath is of white among the stars. He has a brownish muzzle and a white diamond shaped patch on his breast. Sometimes he is brown, or red, or yellow, or even white. Not so wise as the wolf, or so fierce as the panther, yet the black bear has outlived them both. "When in doubt, *run!*" is his motto; and like Descartes, the wise black bear founds his life on the doctrine of doubt. As for the unwise—they are dead. To be sure, even this saving rule of conduct would not keep him alive in these days of repeating rifles, were it not for his natural abilities. A bear can hear a hunter a quarter of a mile away, and scent one for over a mile if the wind be right. He may weigh three hundred pounds and be over two feet wide, yet he will slip like a shadow through tangled underbrush without a sound.

Bear cubs are born in January, after the mother bear has gone into winter quarters, blind and bare and pink, and so small that two of them can be held at once on a man's hand. Bears mate every other year, and the half-grown cubs hibernate with the mother during their second winter.

The black bear is a good swimmer, and may sometimes be seen crossing lonely lakes in the northern woods. At such times, he is an ugly customer to tackle without a gun, as he will swim straight at a canoe and tip it over if possible. A friend of mine, while fishing in Upper Canada, on a sluggish river between two lakes, saw a bear swimming well ahead of the canoe. He began to paddle with all his might to overtake him, but to his surprise seemed to be moving backwards. Looking around, he saw his guide, who was more experienced in bear ways, backing water desperately. Just then, the swimming animal turned his head and saw the canoe. Instantly, the hair on his back bristled and stood up in a long stiff ridge, and he stopped swimming—whereupon my friend found himself instantaneously, automatically, and enthusiastically assisting the guide.

Even where the black bear is common, one may spend a long lifetime without sight or sound of him. There may be half a dozen bear feeding in a berry patch. You may find signs that they are close at hand and all about. Yet no matter how you may hide and skulk and hunt, never a glimpse of one of them will you get. In bear country, you will more often smell the hot, strong, unmistakable scent of a bear who is watching you close at hand, than see the bear himself. In fact, the sight of a wild black bear is an adventure worth remembering.

Personally, I am ashamed to say that, although I have tramped and camped and fished and hunted on both sides of the continent, I have never really seen a bear. Twice I have had glimpses of one. The first time was in what was then the Territory of Washington. I was walking with a friend through a bit of virgin forest. The narrow path was walled in on both sides by impenetrable windbreaks and underbrush. As we suddenly and silently came around a sharp bend, there was a crash through a mass of fallen trees, and I almost saw what caused it. At least I saw the bushes move. Right ahead of us, in the mould of a torn and rotted stump, was a footprint like that of a broad, short, bare human foot. It was none other than the pawmark of Mr. Bear, who is a plantigrade and walks flatfooted. Although I was sorry to miss seeing him, yet I was glad that it was the bear and not the man who had to dive through that underbrush.

Another time, I was camping in Maine. Not far from our tent, which we had cunningly concealed on a little knoll near the edge of a lonely lake, I found a tiny brook, which trickled down a hillside. Although it ran through dense underbrush, it was possible to fish it, and every afternoon I would bring back half a dozen jeweled trout to broil for supper. One day, I had gone farther in than usual, and was standing silently, up to my waist in water and brush, trying to cast over an exasperating bush into a little pool beyond. Suddenly I smelt bear. Not far from me there sounded a very faint crackling in the bushes on a little ridge, about as loud as a squirrel would make. As I leaned forward to look, my knee came squarely against a nest of enthusiastic and able-bodied yellow jackets. Instantly, a cloud of them burst over me like shrapnel, stinging my unprotected face unendurably. As I struck at them with my hand, I caught just one glimpse of a patch of black fur through the brush on the ridge above me. The next second, my hand struck my eyeglasses, and they went spinning into the brush, lost forever, and I was stricken blind. Thereafter, I dived and hopped like a frog through the brush and water, until I came out beyond that yellow jacket barrage. I never saw that bear again. Probably he laughed himself to death.

The black bear is undoubtedly leather-lined, for he will dig up and eat the bulbs of the jack-in-the-pulpit, which affect a human tongue—I speak from knowledge—like a mixture of nitric acid and powdered glass. Moreover, he is the only animal which can swallow the tight-rolled green cigars of the skunk cabbage in the early spring. An entry in my nature notes reads as follows:—

"Only a fool or a bear would taste skunk cabbage."

My lips were blistered and my tongue swollen when I wrote it. The fact that the black bear and the black cat or fisher are the only two mammals which can eat Old Man Quill-Pig, alias porcupine, and swallow his quills, confirms my belief as to the bear's lining. The dog, the lynx, the wild cat, and the wolf have all tried—and died.

Last spring, in northern Pennsylvania, I found myself on the top of a mountain, by the side of one of those trembling bogs locally known as bear sloughs. There I had highly resolved to find the nest of a nearby Nashville warbler, which kept singing its song, which begins like a black-and-white warbler and ends like a chipping sparrow. I did not suppose that there was a bear within fifty miles of me. Suddenly, I came upon a large, quaking aspen tree set back in the woods by the side of the bog. Its smooth bark was furrowed by a score of deep scratches and ridges about five feet from the ground, while above them the tree had apparently been repeatedly chewed. I recognized it as a bear tree. In the spring, and well through the summer, certain trees are selected by all the he-bears of a territory as a signpost whereon they carve messages for friend and foe. No male bear of any real bearhood would think of passing such a tree without cutting his initials wide, deep, and high, for all the world to see.

The first flurries of snow mean bedtime for Bruin. He is not afraid of the cold, for he wears a coat of fur four inches thick over a waistcoat of fat of the same thickness. He has found, however, that rent is cheaper than board. Unless there comes some great acorn year, when the oak trees are covered with nuts, he goes to bed when the snow flies. One of the rarest adventures in woodcraft is the finding of a bear hole where Bruin sleeps rolled up in a big, black ball until spring. It is always selected and concealed with the utmost care, for the black bear takes no chances of being attacked in his sleep. The last bear hole of which I have heard was not far from home. Two friends of mine were shooting in the Pocono Mountains with a dog, about the middle of November, 1914. Suddenly the dog started up a black bear on a wooded slope. After running a short distance, the bear turned and popped into a hole under an overhanging bank. Almost immediately, he started to come out again, growling savagely. I am sorry to say that my friends shot him.

Then they explored the hole, which he was preparing for his winter quarters. It was beautifully constructed. The entrance was under an overhanging bank, shielded by bushes, and it seemed unbelievable that so large an animal could have forced his shoulders through so small a hole. The burrow was jug-shaped, spreading out inside and sloping up, while a dry shelf had been dug out in the bank. This was covered with layers of dry leaves and a big blanket of withered grass. In the top of the bank a tiny hole had been dug, which opened out in some thick bushes and was probably an air hole. Just outside the entrance, a bear had piled an armful of dry sticks, evidently intending, when he had finally entered the hole, to pull them over the entrance and entirely hide it. The bear itself turned out to be a young one. A veteran would have died fighting before giving up the secret of his winter castle.

The opal water was all glimmering green and gold and crimson, as it whirled under overhanging boughs aflame with the fires of fall. The air tasted of frost, and had the color of pale gold. Around sudden curves, through twisted channels, and down gleaming vistas, our canoe followed the crooked stream as it ran through the pine barrens. The woods on either side were glories of color. There was the scarlet of the mountain sumac, with its winged leaves, and the deep purple of the star-leaved sweet gum. Sassafras trees were lemon-yellow or wine-red. The persimmon was the color of gold, while the poison sumac, with its death-pale bark, and venomous leaves upcurled as if ready to sting, flaunted the regal red-and-yellow of Spain.

At last, we beached our canoe in a little grove and landed for lunch. By the edge of the smoky, golden cedar water, in the pure white sand, was a deep footprint, like that made by a baby's bare foot with a pointed heel. I recognized the hand and seal of Lotor, the Washer, who believes firmly in that old proverb about cleanliness. That is about as near, however, as Lotor ever gets to godliness. He is the grizzled gray raccoon, who wears a black mask on his funny, foxy face, and has a ringed tail shaped like a baton, and sets his hind feet flat, like his second cousin the bear, while his menu card covers almost as wide a range. Whatever he eats—frogs, crawfish, chicken, and even fresh eggs and snakes—he always washes. Two, three, and even four times, he rinses and rubs his food if he can find water.

That footprint in the sand carried me back more years than I like to count. It was on the same kind of fall day that I first entered the fastnesses of Rolfe's Woods. First there came Little Woods, close at home, where one could play after school, and where the spotted leaves of the adder's tongue grew everywhere. Then came Big Woods, which required a full Saturday afternoon to do it justice. It was there that I accumulated by degrees the twenty-two spotted turtles, the five young gray squirrels, and the three garter snakes, which gladdened my home.

Far beyond Big Woods was a wilderness of swamps and thickets known to us as Rolfe's Woods. This was only to be visited in company with some of the big boys and on a full holiday. That day, Boots Lockwood and Buck Thompson, patriarchs who must have been all of fourteen years old, were planning to visit these woods. Four of us little chaps tagged along until it was too late to send us back. We found that the perils of the place had not been overstated. In a dark thicket Boots showed us wolf tracks. At least he said they were, and he ought to have known, for he had read "Frank in the Woods," "The Gorilla-Hunters," and other standard authorities on such subjects. Farther on we heard a squalling note, which Buck at once recognized as the scream of a panther. Boots confirmed his diagnosis, and showed the reckless bravery of his nature by laughing so heartily at our scared faces that he had to lean against a tree for some time before he could go on. In later years, I have heard the same note made by a blue jay, a curious coincidence which should have the attention of some of our prominent naturalists.

Finally, we came to a little clearing with a vast oak tree in the centre. As we neared it, suddenly Buck gave a yell and pointed overhead. There on a hollow dead limb crouched a strange beast. It was gray in color, with a black-masked face, and was ten times larger than any gray squirrel, the wildest animal which we had met personally. There was a hasty and whispered consultation between the two leaders, after which Buck announced that the stranger was none other than a Canada lynx, according to him an animal of almost supernatural ferocity and cunning. Furthermore, he stated that he, assisted by Boots, intended to climb the tree and attack said lynx with a club. Our part was to encircle the tree and help Boots if the lynx elected to fight on land instead of aloft. If so be that he sprang on any one of us, the rest were to attack him instantly, before he had time to lap the blood of his victim—a distressing habit which Buck advised us was characteristic of all Canada lynxes.

This masterly plan was somewhat marred by the actions of Robbie Crane. Robbie was of a gentle nature, and one whose manners and ideals were far superior to the rough boys with whom he occasionally consorted. Mrs. Crane said so herself. After reflecting a moment on the lynx's unrestrained and sanguinary traits, he suddenly disappeared down the backtrack with loud sobbings, and never stopped running until he reached home an hour later. Thereafter, our names were stricken from Robbie's calling list by Mrs. Crane.

As Buck, boosted by Boots, started up the tree, the perfidious lynx disappeared in an unsuspected hole beneath a branch, from which he refused to come out in spite of all that Buck and Boots could do. One member, at least, of that hunting party was immensely relieved by his unexpected retreat. It was many years later before I learned that even such masters of woodcraft as Buck and Boots could be mistaken, and that the Canada lynx was really a Connecticut coon.

It was not until recently that I ever met Lotor by daylight. Three years ago, I was walking down a hillside after a sudden November snowstorm. My way led past two gray squirrel nests, well thatched and chinked with the leaves by which they can always be told from crows' nests. From one of them I saw peering down at me the funny face of a coon. When I pounded on the other tree, another coon stared sleepily down at me. Probably the unexpected snowstorm had sent them both to bed in the first lodgings which they could find; or it may be that they had decided to try the open air sleeping rooms of the squirrels rather than the hollow tree houses in which the coon family usually spend their winters.

Sometimes at night you may hear, near the edge of the woods, a plaintive, tremulous call floating from out of the dark trees—"Whoo-oo-oo-oo, whoo-oo-oo-oo." It is one of the night notes of the coon. It sounds almost like the wail of the little screech owl, save that there is a certain animal quality to the note. Moreover, the screech owl will always answer, when one imitates the call, and will generally come floating over on noiseless wings to investigate. The coon, however, instantly detects the imitation and calls no more that night.

Unlike the bears, Mr. and Mrs. Coon and all the little coons, averaging from three to six, hibernate together soon after the first snowstorm of the year. One of the few legends of the long lost Connecticut Indians which I can remember is that of an old Indian hunter, who would appear on my great grandfather's farm in the depths of winter and, after obtaining permission, would go unerringly to one or more coon trees, which he would locate by signs unknown to any white hunter. In each tree, he would find from four to six fat coons, whose fur and flesh he would exchange for gunpowder, tobacco, hard cider, and other necessities of life.

Mr. and Mrs. Coon are good parents. They keep their children with them until the arrival of a new family, which occurs with commendable regularity every spring. A friend of mine once saw a young coon fall into the water from its tree in the depths of a swamp. At the splash, the mother coon came out of the den, forty feet up the trunk, and climbed down to help. Master Coon, wet, shaken, and miserable, managed to get back to the tree trunk and clung there whimpering. Mother Coon gripped him by the scruff of his neck, and marched him up the tree to the den, giving him a gentle nip whenever he stopped to cry.

In spite of his funny face and playful ways, Mr. Coon is a cheerful, desperate, scientific fighter. In a fair fight, or an unfair one for that matter, he will best a dog double his size, and he fears no living animal of his own weight, save only that versatile weasel, the black cat. I became convinced of this one dark November morning many years ago, when I foolishly used to kill animals instead of making friends of them. All night long, with a pack of alleged coon dogs, we had hunted invisible and elusive coons through thick woods. I had scratched myself all over with greenbrier, and while running through the dark, had plunged head first into the coldest known brook on the continent. Four separate times, I had been persuaded by false and flattering words to climb slippery trees after imaginary coons, with a lantern fastened round my neck.

This time my friends assured me there could be no mistake. Both Grip and Gyp, the experts of the pack, had their forepaws against an enormous tulip tree which stood apart from all others. In order that there might be no possible mistake, black Uncle Zeke, the leader of the hunt, who knew most of the coons in those woods by their first names, agreed to "shine" this particular coon. Lighting a lantern, he held it behind his head, staring fixedly up into the tree as he did so. Sure enough, in a minute, far up along the branches gleamed two green spots. Those were the eyes of the coon, staring down at the light. It was impossible to climb this tree, so we built a fire and waited for daylight.

Dawn found us regarding a monster coon crouched in the branches some forty or fifty feet up. Uncle Zeke produced a cherished shotgun. The barrel had once burst, by reason of the muzzle being accidentally plugged with mud, and had been thereafter cut down, so that it was less than a foot in length. In spite of its misfortune, Uncle Zeke assured us that it was still a wonderful shooter. We scattered and gave him a free field. In a properly conducted coon hunt, a coon, like a fox, must be killed by dogs or not at all. Uncle Zeke told us that this one, as soon as he heard the shot, although uninjured, would come down, like Davy Crockett's coon.

Sure enough, when the shot cut through the branches well above the animal, he started slowly down the trunk, head foremost, like a squirrel, and never stopped until he reached a branch some twenty feet above the yelping pack. Then, with hardly a pause, he launched himself right into their midst. As he came through the air, we could see him slashing with his claws, evidently limbering up. He struck the ground, only to disappear in a wave of dogs. In a minute, he fought himself clear, and managed to get his back against the tree. Then followed a great exhibition of scientific fighting. The coon was perfectly balanced on all four feet, and did wonderful execution with his flexible forepaws, armed with sharp, curved claws. He went through that mongrel pack like a light weight champion in a street fight. Ducking, side stepping, slashing and biting fiercely in the clinches, he broke entirely through the circle, and started off at a brisk trot toward the thick woods. The pack followed after him, baying ferociously, but doing nothing more. Not one of them would venture again into close quarters. Though we came back empty-handed, not even Uncle Zeke grudged that coon his life.

The motto of the next sleeper is, "Don't hurry, others will." If you meet in your wanderings a black-and-white animal wearing a pointed nose, a bushy tail, and an air of justified confidence, avoid any altercation with him. The skunk discovered the secret of the gas attack a million years before the Boche. He is one of the best friends of the farmer—and the worst treated. Given a fair chance, every week he will eat several times his weight in mice and insects. Moreover, with the muskrat he contributes divers furs to the market, whose high sounding names disguise their lowly origin. During the coldest part of the winter he retires to his burrow and sleeps fitfully. He is the last to go to bed and the first to get up; and on any warm day in late winter you may see his close-set, alternate, stitch-like tracks in the snow. The black-and-white banner of skunk kind is a huge bushy resplendent tail, sometimes as wide as it is long. At the very tip is set a tuft like the white plume of Henry of Navarre. When it stands straight up, the battle is on, and wise wild folk remove themselves elsewhere with exceeding swiftness. As for the simple—they wish they had.

The armament of this Seventh Sleeper is simple but effective. It consists of two scent glands, located near the base of the tail, which empty into a movable duct or pipe, which can be protruded some distance. Through this duct, by means of large contractile muscles, a stream of liquid musk can be propelled with incredible accuracy, and with a range of from six to ten feet. Moreover the skunk's accurate breech loading and repeating weapon has one device not yet found in any man-made artillery. Each gland, besides the hole for long-range purposes, is pierced with a circle of smaller holes through which the deadly gas can be sprayed in a cloud for work at close quarters. The skunk's battery can be operated over the bow or from port or starboard, but rarely astern.

The liquid musk itself is a clear, golden-yellow fluid full of little bubbles of the devastating gas, and curiously enough is almost identical in appearance with the venom of the rattlesnake. As to its odor, it has been described feelingly as a mixture of perfume musk, essence of garlic, burning sulphur, and sewer gas, raised to the thousandth power. Its effect is very much like that produced by the fumes of ammonia, another animal product, or the mustard gas of modern warfare. It may cause blindness, convulsions, and such constriction and congestion of the breathing passages as even to bring about death. Some individuals and animals, however, seem to be more or less immune to the effects of this secretion. I remember once attending, by invitation, a possum hunt conducted by a number of noted possumists of color. We were accompanied by a bevy of miscellaneous dogs. The possums were generally found wandering here and there among the thickets, or located in low persimmon trees. Every now and then, one of the dogs would bring to bay a strolling skunk. As the skins had a considerable market value, these skunks were regarded as the special prizes of the chase. The hunters dispatched them by a quick blow across the back, which broke the spine. Such a blow paralyzed the muscles and effectually prevented any further artillery practice on the part of the skunk which had received it. Before it could be delivered, both the hunter and the dog were usually exposed to an unerring barrage, which however seemed to cause them no especial inconvenience. Before long every hunter, except myself, had one or more skunks tucked away in his pockets.

It was a long, strong night. Before it was over, I was in some doubt as to whether I had been attending a possum hunt or had taken part in a skunk chase. My family had no doubt whatever on the subject when I reached home the next morning. I was earnestly invited to tarry in the wilderness until such time as I could obtain a complete change of raiment. Thereafter I tried to give my hunting clothes away to the worthy poor.

Said poor, however, would have none of them, and they repose in a lonely grave in a Philadelphia backyard even unto this day.

I saw him last fall, sitting up like a little post in the Half-Moon Lot where the blind blue gentian grows. Every once in a while he would drop down and begin to nibble again, only to stop and sit up stiff and straight on sentry duty. For the gray, grizzled woodchuck is as wary as he is fat. Watchfulness is the price of his life.

Once I spied him far out in a clover patch, nibbling away at the pink sweet blossoms as I passed along the road. At the bar way, a chipmunk leaped into the wall with a sharp squeak. Without even stopping to raise his head, Mr. Woodchuck scuttled through the clover, and dived into his burrow. It was a bit of animal teamwork such as takes place when a fox or a deer uses a faraway crow or a jay as a picket, and dashes away at its warning of the coming of an enemy.

Soon afterwards, I was on my way to a spring down in the pasture. As I passed near a stone wall half hidden in a tangle of chokecherries and bittersweet, there was a piercing whistle, followed by a scrambling and a scuffling as the woodchuck dived down among the stones, and I understood why, below Mason and Dixon's Line, he is always called the "whistle pig." It is a good name, for he whistles, and he is certainly like a little pig in that he eats and eats and eats until he seems mostly quivering paunch. According to the farmers of Connecticut, he eats to get strength enough to dig, and then digs to get an appetite to eat, and so passes his life in a vicious circle of eating and digging and digging and eating. In spite of his unwieldy weight, the woodchuck is a bitter, brave fighter when fight he must.

I once watched a bull terrier named Paddy tackle a big chuck near a shallow brook. Round and round the dog circled, trying for the fatal throat hold. Round and round whirled the brave old chuck, chattering with his great chisel-like teeth, which could bite through dog hide and dog flesh and bone just as easily as they gnawed through stolen apples. Every once in a while, Paddy would clinch, but the woodchuck saved himself every time by hunching his neck down between his round shoulders and punishing the dog so terribly with his sharp teeth that the latter would at last retreat, yelping with pain. They would whirl in circles, and roll over and over in the clinches; but always the old chuck would be found with his squat figure on its legs at the end of each round. His thick grizzled coat was more of a protection, too, than the thin skin of the shorthaired terrier.

At last both of them were tired out. As if by agreement, both drew back and lay down, panting and watching each other's every movement like two boxers. Finally, the woodchuck, who was nearer the brook, began to drag himself along until he reached the edge of the water. Then he lowered his head, still watching his opponent, and sucked in deep, cool, satisfying drinks.

It was too much for Paddy. He started for the brook also. The old chuck stopped drinking, and pulled himself together; but Paddy wanted water, not blood. In a moment he had his nose in the brook. There the two lay, not a couple of yards apart, and drank until they could drink no more.

The whistle pig was the first out. Slowly and watchfully he waddled away from the brook and toward the stonewall, that refuge of all hunted little animals. Paddy gave a fierce growl, but the water tasted too good, and he stayed for another long drink. Then he darted out after the woodchuck, barking ferociously all the time, as if he could hardly wait to begin the battle again. The woodchuck watched him steadily, ready to stop and fight at any moment.

Somehow, although Paddy barked and growled and rushed at his retreating opponent with exceeding fierceness, there were always a few yards between them, until Mr. Chuck disappeared at last down between two great stones in the wall. Then indeed Paddy dashed in, and growled, and tore up the turf, and stuck his nose deep down between the stones, and told the world all the terrible things he would do to that woodchuck if he could only catch him. From the bowels of the old wall, between barks, sounded now and then the muffled but defiant whistle of the unconquered whistle pig.

Finally, Paddy, with an air of having done all that could be expected, gave some fierce farewell barks and trotted off toward the farmhouse.

Some people claim to have dug woodchucks out of their holes. Personally, I believe that it is about as easy to dig a woodchuck out of its hole as it is to catch a squirrel in its tree. They have a network of holes, and have a habit of starting digging on their own account when molested, and sealing up the new hole after them, so that they leave no trace.

Once, in company with another amateur naturalist, we tried to dig an old chuck out of its burrow. After first stopping up all the spare holes we could find, the naturalist dug and dug and dug and dug. Then we enlisted two other men, and they dug and dug and dug. After a while, we came to a mass of great boulders. Then we pressed into service a yoke of oxen, and they tugged and tugged and tugged. Said digging and tugging and tugging and digging lasted the half of a long summer day. All together, it was an exceeding great digging—but we never got that woodchuck.

In September and October, the woodchuck devotes all of his time to eating. The consequence is that, by the time the first frost comes, he is a big gray bag of fat. Mr. Woodchuck does not believe in storing up food in his burrow, like the chipmunk. He prefers to be the storehouse. Soon after the first frost, he disappears in his hole, and far down underground, at the end of a network of intersecting passages, rolls himself up in a round, warm ball, and sleeps until spring.

According to the legend, on Candlemas, or Ground-Hog Day,—which comes on February second,—he peeps out, and, if he can see his shadow, goes in again for six more weeks of cold weather. So far this day has not yet been made a legal holiday. It probably will be some time, along with Columbus Day, Labor Day, and other equally important days. I will not vouch for the fact that the weather depends on the shadow; but there is no doubt that the woodchuck does come out of his burrow in a February thaw and looks around, as his tracks prove; but he is not interested in his shadow. No indeed! What he comes out for is to look for the future Mrs. Woodchuck, and when he finds her he goes in again.

Sometimes, you read in nature books that the woodchuck is good to eat. Don't believe it. I ought to know. I ate one once. Anyone is welcome to my share of the world's supply of woodchucks. When I camped out as a boy, we had to eat everything that we shot: and one summer I ate a part of a woodchuck, a crow, a green heron, and a blue jay. The chuck was about in the crow's class.

We humans have different feelings toward the different Sleepers. One may respect the bear, and have a certain tempered regard for the coon, or even the skunk. Everyone, however, loves that confiding, gentle little Sleeper, the striped chipmunk— "Chippy Nipmunk," as certain children of my acquaintance have named him. He is that little squirrel who lives in the ground and has two big pockets in his cheeks. Sometimes, in the fall, you may think that he has the mumps. Really it is only acorns. He can carry four of them in each cheek. Once I met a greedy chipmunk who had his pockets so full of nuts that he could not enter his own burrow. Although he tried with his head sideways, and even upside down, he could not get in. When he saw me coming, he rapidly removed two hickory nuts from which he had nibbled the sharp points at each end, and popped into his hole, leaving the nuts high, but not dry, outside. When I carried them off, he stuck his head out of the hole, and shouted, "Thief! Thief!" after me in chipmunk language, so loudly that, in order not to be arrested, I carried them back again.

Almost the first wild animal of my acquaintance was the chipmunk. During one of my very early summers, probably the fourth or fifth, a wave of chipmunks swept over the old farm where I happened to be. They swarmed everywhere, and every stonewall seemed to be alive with them. It was probably one of the rare chipmunk migrations, which, although denied by some naturalists, actually do occur.

Chippy usually goes to bed in late October, and sleeps until late March. He takes with him a light lunch of nuts and seeds, in case he may wake up and be hungry during the long night. Moreover, these come in very handy along about breakfast time, for when he gets up there is little to eat. Then, too, he is very busy during those early spring weeks. In the first place, he has to sing his spring song for hours. It is a loud, rolling "Chuck-a-chuck-a-chuck," almost like a birdsong, and Chippy is very proud of it. Then, too, he has to find a suitable Miss Chipmunk and persuade her to become Mrs. Chipmunk, all of which takes a great deal of time. So the nuts, which he stores up, are probably intended rather for an early breakfast than a late supper.

An Indian writer tells how the boys of his tribe used to take advantage of the chipmunk's spring serenade. The first warm day in March they would all start out armed with bows and arrows, and at the nearest chipmunk hole one would imitate the loud chirrup of the chipmunk. Instantly, every chipmunk within hearing would pop out of his hole and join the chorus, until sometimes as many as fifty would be singing at the same time, too busily to dodge the blunt arrows of the boy hunters.

Besides his song, the chipmunk has another high pitched note, and an alarm squeal which he gives as he dives into his burrow. There are two phases of Eastern chipmunks, the Northern and the Southern, besides the Oregon, the painted, and the magnificent golden chipmunk of the West. All of them have the same dear, gentle ways.

When I was a boy, a chipmunk was a favorite pet. Flying squirrels were too sleepy, red squirrels too restless, and gray squirrels too bitey for petting purposes. Chippy is easily tamed, and moreover does not have to be kept in a cage, which is no place for any wild animal. I knew one once, who used to go to school in a boy's pocket every day; and he behaved quite as well as the boy, which is not saying much. Sometimes, he would come out and sit on the desk beside the boy's book, so as to help him over the particularly hard places.

The chipmunk, like most of the Sleepers, has a varied diet. He eats all kinds of nuts and weed seeds, and also has a pretty taste in mushrooms. It was a chipmunk who once taught me the difference between a good and a bad mushroom. I saw him sitting on a stump, nibbling what seemed to be a red russula, which tastes like red pepper and acts like an emetic if one is foolish enough to swallow much of it. When I came near, he ran away, leaving his lunch behind. On tasting the mushroom, I found that although it was a red russula, it was not the *emetica*, and I learned to recognize the delicious *alutacea*.

Sometimes, sad to say, Chippy eats forbidden food. A friend of mine found him once on a low limb, nibbling a tiny, green grass snake. The chipmunk had eaten about half of the snake, when he suddenly stopped and let the remainder drop, and then sat and reflected for a full minute. At the end of that time he became actively ill, and after losing all of that fresh snake lunch, scampered away, an emptier, if not a wiser, chipmunk.

In spite of his gentle ways, Chippy lives in a world of enemies. Hawks, snakes, cats, boys, and dogs, all are his foes. More than all the rest put together, however, he fears the devilish red weasel, which runs him down relentlessly above and below the ground alike. Only in the water has the chipmunk a chance to escape. Although the weasel can hold him for a few yards, yet in a long swim the chipmunk will draw away so far from his pursuer that he will generally escape. Underground, if given a few seconds' time, he also escapes by a method known to a number of the underground folk. Dashing through a series of the main burrows, he runs into a side gallery, and instantly walls himself in so neatly that his pursuer rushes past without suspecting his presence.

For many years, one of the out-of-door problems to which I was unable to find the answer was how a chipmunk could dig a burrow and leave no trace of any fresh earth. I examined scores of new chipmunk holes, but never found the least trace of fresh earth near the entrance. His secret is to start at the other end. This sounds like a joke, but it is exactly what he does. He will run a shaft for many feet, coming up in some convenient thicket or beneath the slope of an overhanging bank. All the earth will be taken out through the first hole, which is then plugged up. This accounts for the heaps of fresh earth, which I have frequently seen near chipmunk colonies, but with no burrow anywhere in sight.

The Band was on the march. The evening before, at story time, Sergeant Henny-Penny and Corporal Alice-Palace had listened spellbound while the Captain told them of the adventures of trustful Chippy-Nipmunk when he tried to get change for a horse chestnut from Mr. G. Squirrel, who it seems was of a grasping and over-reaching disposition, and how Chippy wrote home about the transaction signing himself "Butternutly yours." The story had made such a sensation that the flattered Captain had promised, on the next day, which was a half holiday, to take the whole Band up to Chipmunk Hill, where old Mr. Prindle had named and tamed a chipmunk colony.

Late afternoon found them plodding up the grass grown road, which led to the lonely little house on top of the hill, where Mr. Prindle had lived since days before which the memory of the Band ran not. They found the old man seated on the porch in a great Boston rocker, and glad enough to see them all. The Captain introduced them in due form, from First Lieutenant Trottie down to Corporal Alice-Palace.

" 'T ain't everybody," said Mr. Prindle, pulling Second Lieutenant Honey's ear reflectively, "that would climb five miles uphill to see an old man. How would a few fried cakes and some cider go?"

There was an instantaneous vote in favor of this resolution, in which Alice-Palace's good time noise easily soared like a siren whistle above all the other expressions of assent.

"Be careful and don't swallow the holes," Mr. Prindle warned them a few moments later, as he brought out a big panful of brownish-red, spicy fried cakes cooked in twisted rings.

The Band promised to use every precaution, and there was an adjournment of all other business until the pan and the pitcher were alike empty.

"Are your chipmunks still alive?" queried the Captain, as they all sat down on the vast, squatty legged settee next to Mr. Prindle's rocker.

"Yes, indeed," replied the latter, "they've been with me nigh on to four years now."

Alice-Palace's eyes became very big.

"Not Chippy-Nipmunk?" she whispered to the Captain.

"Exactly," replied that official, "and then some."

Thereafter, at Mr. Prindle's suggestion, they all sat stony-still and mousy-quiet while he made a funny little hissing, whistling noise. From under the porch there came a scurrying rush, and the two bright eyes of a big striped chipmunk popped up over the edge of the porch step. A minute later, from two holes in a nearby bank, two other chipmunks dashed out. They all had ashy-gray backs, with five stripes of such dark brown as to look almost like black. Their tails had a black, white-tipped fringe, while the gray color of the back changed into clear orange-brown on their flanks and legs.

"This one is James," announced Mr. Prindle, as the first chipmunk hurried across the porch toward his chair. "His full name is James William Francis," he explained, "after a second cousin of mine who looked a good deal like him. I generally call him James for short. The other two are Nip and Tuck," he went on. "Old Bill will be along in a minute. You see," he continued, "he's an old bachelor and lives all by himself quite a ways off."

"What about James?" inquired Honey.

"He's been a widower," said Mr. Prindle, sadly, "ever since his wife stayed out one day to get a good look at a hawk."

As he spoke, another chipmunk came around the end of the porch and hastened to join the other three.

"Here's Bill now," announced Mr. Prindle.

Then, the old man reached into his pocket and took out a handful of butternuts and gave two to each of the Band.

"Hold one in your closed hand and the other between your thumb and finger where they can see it," he advised them.

A moment later, there was a chorus of delighted squeals. Each chipmunk had run up and taken the nut which was in sight, and was burrowing and scrabbling with soft little paws and sniffling little noses into four sets of clenched fingers, in an attempt to secure the other hidden nuts. When the last of them had disappeared, looking as if he had an attack of mumps, the Band thanked Mr. Prindle and started for home.

"Butternutly yours," quoted Alice-Palace as they hurried down the long hill.

Have you ever dreamed of writing a wonderful poem, and then waked up and found that you had forgotten it; or, worse still, that it wasn't wonderful at all? That is what happened to me the other night. All that was left of the lost masterpiece was the following alleged verse:—

> After dark everybody's house
> Belongs to the little brown Flittermouse.

I admit that the mystery and pathos and beauty which that verse seemed to have in dreamland have some way evaporated in daylight. So as I can't give to the world any poetry in praise of my friend the Flittermouse, I must do what I can for him in prose. In the first place, his everyday name is Bat. Our forebears knew him as the flying or "flitter" mouse. Probably, too, he is the original of the Brownie, that ugly brown elf that used to flit about in the twilight.

He is perhaps the best equipped of all of our mammals, for he flies better than any bird, is a strong though unwilling swimmer, and is also fairly active on the ground. In addition, he has such an exquisite sense of feeling that he is able to fly at full speed in the dark, steering his course and instantly avoiding any obstacle by the mere feel of the air currents. In fact, the bat's whole body, including the ribs and edges of its wings, may be said to be full of eyes. These are highly developed nerve endings, which are so sensitive that they are instantly aware of the presence of any body met in flight, by the difference in the air pressure.

As early as 1793, an Italian naturalist found that a blinded bat could fly as well as one with sight. They were able to avoid all parts of a room, and even to fly through silken threads stretched in such a manner as to leave just space enough for them to pass with their wings expanded. When the threads were placed closer together, the blind bats would contract their wings in order to pass between them without touching.

An English naturalist put wax over a bat's closed eyes and then let it loose in a room. It flew under chairs, of which there were twelve in the room, without touching anything, even with the tips of its wings. When he attempted to catch it, the bat dodged; nor could it be taken even when resting, as it seemed to feel with its wings the approach of the hand stretched out to seize it.

When it comes to flying, the bat is the swallow of the night. Sometimes, it may be confused with a chimney swift at twilight, but it can always be told by its dodging, lonely flight, while the swifts fly in companies and without zigzagging through the air. It is doubtful whether even the swallow or the swiftest of the hawks, such as the sharp-shinned or the duck hawk, perhaps the fastest bird that flies, can equal the speed of the great hoary bat. Moreover, the flight of the bat is absolutely silent. He may dart and turn a foot away from you, but you will hear absolutely nothing. A hoary bat, the largest of all the family, has been seen to overtake and fly past a flock of migrating swallows, while a red bat has been watched carrying four young clinging to her, which together weighed more than she did, and yet she flew and hunted and captured insects in midair as usual. There is no bird which can give such an exhibition of strong flying. The hoary bat has even been found on the Bermuda Islands in autumn and early winter. As these islands are five hundred and forty storm-swept miles from the nearest land, this is evidence of an extraordinarily high grade of wing power.

When it comes to personal habits, bats of all kinds are perhaps the most useful mammals that we have. No American bat eats anything but insects, and insects of the most disagreeable kind, such as cockroaches, mosquitoes, and June bugs. A house bat has been seen to eat twenty-one June bugs in a single night; while another young bat would eat from thirty-four to thirty-seven cockroaches in the same time, beginning this commendable work before it was two months old. Moreover, bats do not bring into houses any noxious insects, like bedbugs or lice, despite their bad reputation. They are unfortunately afflicted with numerous parasites, but none of them are of a kind to attack man. All bats are great drinkers, and twice a day skim over the nearest water, drinking copiously on the wing. Sometimes, where trout are large enough, bats fall victims to their drinking habits, being seized on the wing like huge moths by leaping trout, as they approach the water to drink.

Bats also feed twice a day at regular periods, once at sundown and once at sunrise, always capturing and eating their insect food on the wing. Some of them have a curious habit of using a pouch, which is made of the membrane stretched between their hind legs, as a kind of net to hold the captured insect until it can be firmly gripped and eaten. In this same pouch, the young are carried as soon as they are born, and until they are strong enough to nurse. After that, like young jumping mice, they cling to the teats of the mother bat, and are carried everywhere in this way. When they get too large to be so conveyed in comfort, the mother bat hangs them up in some secret place until her return.

Moreover, a mother bat is just as devoted to her babies as any other mammal. She takes entire charge of them, with never any help from the father bat. Young bats are blind at birth, but their eyes open on the fifth day, and on the thirteenth day the baby bat no longer clings to its mother, but roosts beside her. The bat has from two to four young, depending on the species. Most young bats can fly and forage for themselves when they are about three months old, although the silvery bat begins to fly when it is three weeks old. No bat makes a nest.

Titian Peale, of Philadelphia, in an early natural history, tells a story of a boy who, in 1823, caught a young red bat and took it home. Three hours later, in the evening, he started to take it to the museum, carrying it in his hand. As he passed near the place where it was caught, the mother bat appeared and followed the boy for two squares, flying around him and finally lighting on his breast, until the boy allowed her to take charge of her little one.

The bat has but few enemies. They are occasionally caught by owls, probably taken unawares, or when hanging in some dark tree. In fact, virtually the only enemies a bat has are fur lice, which breed upon them in enormous quantities. It is this misfortune, and the fact that a bat has a strong rank smell like that of a skunk, which keeps it from being popular as a pet.

A friend of mine once, however, kept a little brown bat, which had been drowned out from a tree by a thunderstorm, for a long time under a sieve as a pet. The bat became tame and would accept food, and it was most interesting to see the deft, speedy way in which he husked millers and other minute insects, rejecting their wings, skinning their bodies, and devouring the flesh only after it had been prepared entirely to its liking. He would wash himself with his tongue and his paw, like a cat, using the little thumbnail at the bend of his wing, and stretching the rubbery membrane into all kinds of shapes, until it seemed as if he would tear it in his zeal for cleanliness.

A bat always alights first by catching the little hooks on its wings. As soon as it has a firm grip with these, it at once turns over, head downward, and hangs by the long, recurved nails of the hind feet, and in this position sleeps through the daylight. It sleeps through the winter in the top of some warm steeple or, far more often than we suspect, in dark corners of our houses, and sometimes in hollow trees and deserted buildings and caves. Only when caught by the cold does the bat hibernate. Often it migrates like the birds.

One of the strangest things about the flitter mouse is its voice. It is a penetrating, shrill squeak, so high that many people cannot hear it at all. The chirp of a sparrow is about five octaves above the middle E of the piano, while the cry of the bat is a full octave above that. In England there is a saying that no person more than forty years old can hear the cry of a bat. This is founded probably on the fact that the ears of many of us, especially as we approach middle age, are unable to distinguish sounds more than four octaves above middle E. Some naturalists believe that the shrill squeak which most of us do hear is only one of many notes of the bat, and that the various species have different calls, like those of birds, and probably even have a love song during the mating season, in late August or early September, which can never be heard by human ears.

Most bats found in the Eastern States are either large brown house bats, one of two kinds of little brown bats, black bats, red or tree bats, pigmy bats, or, last, largest and most beautiful of all, hoary bats. The big brown bat, or house bat, is the commonest. This is the last of the bats to come out in the evening, for each has a certain fixed hour when it begins to hunt, which varies only with the light. When the big brown bat starts, the twilight has almost turned to dark.

The two kinds of little brown bat, Leconte's and Say's, cannot be told apart in flight. Both of them are much smaller than the big brown bat, and the ear of a Leconte's bat barely reaches the end of the nose, while that of a Say's bat is considerably longer. All bats have large ears, each of which contains a curious inner ear known as the "antitragus." Both of these little bats are country bats and prefer caves and hollow trees to houses and outbuildings.

The black bat can be told from all other American bats by its deep black-brown color touched with silvery white. This bat likes to hunt and hawk over water, skimming across ponds like swallows. Some of the black bat colonies, or "batteries," are very large, one by actual count including 9,640 bats.

Next comes the Georgia pigmy bat, so called to distinguish it from the very rare New York pigmy bat. This little bat can be told by its small size, for it is the smallest of all of our eastern bats, by its yellowish pale color, and especially by its flight, which is weak and fluttering, like that of a large butterfly.

The red bat is a tree bat, spending the daytime in the foliage of trees, and rarely, if ever, being found in caves or houses. It can be told at a glance by its red color. It is the greatest of all the bats except the last, the hoary bat, the largest of them all, with a wingspread of from fifteen to seventeen inches. This great bat soars high, well above the tree tops, where it can prey upon the high flying great moths. It is one of the most beautiful, as well as the rarest, of our bats, being found in the East only in the spring or fall migration. It wears a magnificent furry coat as beautiful as that of the silver fox, but, like all of its race, it is cursed with the homeliest face ever worn by an animal. It is this hobgoblin face, which, in spite of a blameless life and useful habits, makes the flitter mouse, whatever its species, universally hated.

However, handsome is as handsome does, and the boy who kills a bat has killed one of our most useful animals and deserves to be bitten by all the mosquitoes, and bumped by all the June bugs, and crawled over by all the cockroaches, and to have his clothes corrupted by all the moths, that the dead bat would have eaten if it had been allowed to live.

After I had supposedly finished this chapter, I was reading it aloud at the dinner table to the defenseless Band, one Sunday afternoon about two o 'clock, on a freezing day in December. Just as I was in the midst of the masterpiece, one of my audience suddenly woke up and said, "There's a bat!" Sure enough, outside, in the glass-enclosed porch, was flying a large brown house bat. Back and forth it went through the freezing air, as swiftly as if it were summer. I was much touched by this beautiful tribute to my authorship, and went out and managed to catch my visitor when he alighted. The bat, however, was ungrateful enough to bite the hand that had praised him, and I will end this account by writing of knowledge that a bat's tiny teeth are as sharp as needles and that he is always willing to use them.

Not dangerous like the skunk, or brave like the raccoon, or big like the bear, the least of the Sleepers is the best looking of them all. Shy and solitary, the gentle little jumping mouse is as dainty as he looks. His fur is lead, overlaid with gold deepening to a dark brown on the back, and like the deer mouse he wears a snowy silk waistcoat and stockings. His strength is in his powerful crooked hind legs, and his length in his silky tail, which occupies five of his eight inches. Given one jump ahead of any foe that runs, springs, flies, or crawls, and Mr. Jumping Mouse is safe. He patters through the grass by the edge of thickets and weed patches, like any other mouse, until alarmed. Then with a bound he shoots high into the air, in a leap that will cover from two to twelve feet. It is in this that his long tail plays its part. In a graceful curve, with tip upturned, it balances and guides him through the air in a jump which will cover over forty times his own length, equivalent to a performance of two hundred and forty feet by a human jumper. The instant he strikes, the jumper soars away again like a bird, at right angles to his first jump, and zigzags here and there through the air, so fast and so far as to baffle even the swift hawk and the dogged weasel.

Every day, Mr. Jumping Mouse washes and polishes his immaculate self, and draws his long silky tail through his mouth until every hair shines. Mrs. Jumping Mouse is a good mother, and never deserts her babies. If alarmed while feeding them, she will spring through the air with from three to five of them clinging to her for dear life, and carry them safely through all her series of lofty leaps.

The first frost rings the bedtime bell for the jumping mouse. Three feet underground he builds a round nest of dried grass, and lines it with feathers, hair, and down. Then he rolls himself into a round bundle, which he ties up with two wraps of his long tail, and goes to sleep until spring. Of all the Sleepers he is the soundest. Dig him up and he shows no sign of life; but if brought in to a fire, he wakes up and becomes his own lively self once more. Put him out in the cold, and he rolls up and falls asleep again.

One of the Band, who holds high office, is by way of being a naturalist instead of an explorer or an aviator, as he originally intended. Last summer, in a bit of dried-up marshland near the roadside, he heard strange rustlings. On investigating, he found a family of young jumping mice moving through the grass and feeding on the buds of alder bushes. They were quite tame, and as they ran out on the ends of the branches, he had a good view of them and finally managed to catch one by the end of his long tail. The mouse bit the boy, but did not even draw blood. Afterwards, he seemed to become tamer, although shaking continually. Given a bit of bread, he sat up and nibbled it like a little squirrel; but even as he ate he suddenly had a spasm of fright and died. This death from fright occurs among a number of the more highly strung of the mice folk, even when they seem to have become perfectly tame. This same young naturalist observed another jumping mouse, which, contrary to all the books, took to the water when pursued, and swam nearly as expertly as a muskrat.

So endeth the Chronicle of the Seven Sleepers.

XII

DRAGON'S BLOOD

*Then Sigurd went his way and roasted the heart of Fafnir
on a rod. And when he tasted the blood, straightway he wot
the speech of every bird of the air.*

It takes longer nowadays. Yet the years are well
spent. There is a strange indescribable happiness that comes with the knowledge of the
bird notes. As for the songs—they are not only among
the joys of life, but they bring with them many other
happinesses. Even as I write, the memory of many of
them comes back to me: wind-swept hilltops; white
sand dunes against a blue, blue sea; singing rows of pine
trees marching miles and miles through the barrens;
jade-green pools; crooked streams of smoky-brown
water; lonely islands; orchid-haunted marshlands; far
journeyings and good fellowship with others who have

learned the Way—these are but a few of them. Let me entreat you to leave the narrow in-door days and wander far afield before it be too late.

> Come sit beside the weary way
> And hear the angels sing.

Ride with Aucassin into the greenwood. There perchance, as happed to him, you will see the green grass grow and listen to the sweet birds sing and hear some good word.

To him who will but listen there are adventures in birdsongs anywhere, any time, and any season. It was but last winter that I found myself again in the dawn-dusk facing a defiant hickory, armed only with an axe. Let me recommend to every man who is worried about his body, his soul, or his estate during the winter months, that he buy or borrow a well-balanced axe and cut down and cut up a few trees for firewood. As he forces the tingling iced oxygen into every cell of his lungs, he will find that he is taking a new view of life and love and debt and death, and other perplexing and perennial topics.

Quite recently I read a journal that a young minister kept, back in the fifties. One entry especially appealed to me.

"Decided this morning that I was not the right man for this church. Chopped wood for two hours in Colonel Hewitt's woodlot. Decided that this was the church for me and that I was the man for this church."

On this particular morning, I heard once more the wild dawn song of the Carolina wren, full of liquid bell-like overtones. As I listened, my mind went back to another wren song. I had been hunting for the nest of a yellow palm warbler in a little gully in the depths of a northern forest. The blood ran down my face from the fierce bites of the black flies, and the mosquitoes stung like fire. Suddenly, from the side of the tiny ravine, began a song full of ringing, glassy notes such as one makes by running a wet finger rapidly on the inside of a thin glass finger bowl. Listening, I forgot that I was wet and tired and hungry and bitten and stung. For the first time I listened to the song of the winter wren. For years I had met this little bird along the sides of brooks in the winter and running in and out of holes and under stones like a mouse; but today to me it was no longer a tiny bird. It was the voice of the untamed, unknown northern woods. It is hard to make any notation of the song. It flowed like some ethereal stream filled with little bubbles of music which broke in glassy tinkling sprays of sound over the undercurrent of the high vibrating melody itself. The song seemed to have two parts. The first ended in a contralto phrase, while the second soared like a fountain into a spray of tinkling trills. Through it all ran a strange unearthly dancing lilt, such as the fairy songs must have had, heard by wandering shepherds at the edge of the green fairy hills. At its very height the melody suddenly ceased, and once again I dropped back into a workaday, mosquito-ridden world, with ten miles between me and my camp.

On that day I found two of the almost unknown, feather-lined nests of the yellow palm warbler, and climbed up to the jewel casket of a bay-breasted warbler, and was shown the cherished secret of a Nashville warbler's nest deep hidden in the sphagnum moss of a little tussock in the middle of a pathless morass. Yet my great adventure was the song of the winter wren.

It was under quite different circumstances that I last heard the best winter singer of all. Never was there a more discouraging day for a collector of birdsongs. The year was dying of rheumy age. On the trees still hung a few dank, blotched leaves, while the sodden ground plashed under foot and a leaden mist of rain covered everything. Yet at the edge of the very first field that I started to cross, a strange call cut through the fog, and I glimpsed a large black-and-white bird crossing the meadow with the dipping up-and-down flight of a woodpecker. It was the hairy woodpecker, the big brother of the more common downy, and a bird that usually loves the depths of the woods. Hardly had it alighted on a wild-cherry tree, when an English sparrow flew up from a nearby ash dump and attacked the new comer. The harassed woodpecker flew to the next tree and the next, but was driven on and away each time by the sparrow, until finally, with another rattling call, it flew back to the woods from whence it had come. A moment later a starling alighted on the same tree, unmolested by its compatriot.

I followed the fields to a nearby patch of woods. It is small and bounded on all sides by crowded roads, but at all times of the year I find birds there. As I reached the edge of the trees, white-skirted juncos flew up in front of me. Mingled with their sharp notes, like the clicking of pebbles, came the gentle whisper of the white-throated sparrow, and from a nearby thicket one of them gave its strange minor song. For its length I know of no minor strain in bird music that is sweeter. Like the little silver flute trill of the pink-beaked field sparrow, and the lovely contralto notes of the bluebird who from mid-sky calls down, "Faraway, faraway, faraway," the song of the white-throated sparrow is tantalizingly brief and simple in its phrasing. Up in Canada the guides call the bird the "widow woman." Usually its song, except in the spring, is incomplete and apt to flatten a little on some of the notes; but today it rang through the rain as true and compelling as when it wakes me, from the syringa and lilac bushes outside my sleeping porch, some May morning.

Through the dripping boughs I pressed far into the very center of the wood. In a tangle of greenbrier sounded a series of sharp irritating chips, and a cardinal, blood-red against the leaden sky, perched himself on a bough of a hornbeam sapling. As I watched him sitting there in the cold rain, he seemed like some bird of the tropics which had flamed his way north and would soon go back to the blaze of sun and riot of color where he belonged. Yet the cardinal grosbeak stays with us all winter, and I have seen four of the vivid males at a time, all crimson against the white snow. Today he looked down upon me, and without any warning suddenly began to sing his full song in a whisper. "Wheepl, wheepl, wheepl," he whistled with a mellow and woodwind note; and again, a full tone lower, "Wheepl, wheepl, wheepl." Then he sang a lilting double-note song, "Chu-wee, chu-wee, chu-wee," ending with a ringing whistle, "Whit, whit, whit, teu, teu, teu," and then ran them together, "Whit-teu, whit-teu, whit-teu." As his lovely dove-colored mate flitted jealously through the thicket, he tactfully and smackingly cried, "Kiss, kiss, kiss," and dived into the bushes to join her. Again and again he ran through his little repertoire, so low that thirty feet away he could hardly be heard. Leaden clouds and dank mists might cover the earth, but life would always be worth the living so long as one could find snatches of jeweled songs like that sung to me by the cardinal. As I started homeward under the dripping sky, crimson against the dark green of a cedar tree, my friend called his goodbye to me in one last long ringing note.

Late that afternoon the rain stopped, the clouds rolled back, and in the west the sky was a mass of flame, with pools of sapphire-blue and rose-red cloud. Above, in a stretch of pure cool apple-green, floated the newest of new moons. As the afterglow ebbed, one by one all the wondrous tints merged into a great band of amber that barred the dark for long. Just before it faded in the last moments of the twilight, there shuddered across the evening air the sweetest, saddest note that can be heard in all winter music. It was a tremolo, wailing little cry that always makes me think of the children the pyxies stole, who can be heard now and again in the twilight, or before dawn, calling, calling vainly for one long gone. In the dim light in a nearby tree, I could see the ear tufts of the little red-brown screech owl. Like the beat of unseen wings, his voice trembled again and again through the air, and answering him, I called him up to within six feet of me. Around and around my head he flew like a great moth, his soft muffled wings making not the faintest breath of sound, until at last he drifted away into the dark.

That night the temperature rose, until the very breath of spring seemed to be in the air; and early the next morning, before even the faint glimmer of the dawn-dusk had shown, I was awakened by hearing a croon so soft and sweet that it ran for long through my dreams without waking me. Again and again it sounded, like the singing ripple of a trout brook or the happy little cradle song that a mother ruffed grouse makes when she broods her leaf-brown chicks. I recognized the love song of the little owl, months before its time—a song which belongs to the nights when the air is full of spring scents and hyla calls.

Perhaps the singer was the same bird who visited Sergeant Henny-Penny one Christmas night. During the day the Band had taken a most successful birdwalk. We had seen and heard some twenty different kinds of birds; heard the white-breasted nuthatch sing his spring song, "Quee-quee-quee," as a Christmas carol for us; met a red fox trotting sedately through the snow, and altogether had a most adventurous day. That evening

I was reading in front of the fire when from Sergeant Henny-Penny's room came an S.O.S. "Fathie, come quick, there's a nangel flyin' around my room," he called.

I hurried, for angels flying or sitting are rarely scored on my bird lists. When I reached the room, Henny-Penny had burrowed so far under the bedclothes that it seemed doubtful if he would ever reach the surface again. When I switched on the light, at first I could see nothing, and I began to be afraid that the "nangel" had escaped through the open window. Finally on the picture moulding I spied the celestial visitor. It was a screech owl of the red phase,—they may be either red or gray,—and when I came near it snapped its beak fiercely, to the terror of the Sergeant under the clothes. With a quick jump I managed to catch it. At first it puffed up its feathers and pretended to be very fierce, but at last it snuggled into my hand and was with difficulty persuaded to fly out again into the cold night.

Another singer of the night is of course the whip-poorwill. When I lived farther out in the country than I do now, for two successive years I was awakened at two o'clock in the morning by a whippoorwill passing north and singing in the nearby woods. The third year he broke all records by alighting on my lawn at sunset in late April. There, under a pink dogwood tree which stood like a statue of spring, he sang for ten minutes. Only once before have I ever heard a whippoorwill sing in the daylight. Once at high noon in the pine barrens, one burst out so loud and ringingly that the pine warbler stopped his trilling and the prairie warbler his seven wire-thin notes which run up the scale. It was as uncanny as when the Lone Wolf gave tongue to the midnight hunting chorus for Mowgli, at the edge of the jungle by day.

Now, when I live nearer civilization, and alas! farther from the birds, I have to travel far to hear whippoorwills. One hour and eleven minutes from my office in time, thirty-seven miles in space, but a whole life away in peace and happiness and rest, I have a little cabin in the heart of the barrens. There in spring I sleep swinging in a hammock above a great bush of mountain laurel, ghost-white against the smoky water of the stream.

Below me in the marsh, where the pitcher plants bloom among the sweet pepper and blueberry bushes, is a pitch pine sapling bent almost into a circle. Sometimes my friends cut exploration paths through the bush or, in the winter, search for firewood, but no one is ever allowed to touch that bent tree. There some spring night, as a little breeze, heavy with the scent of white azalea and creamy magnolia blossoms, sways me back and forth, from the bent tree showing dimly in the moonlight through the tree trunks, the whippoorwill perches himself, lengthwise always, and sings and sings. Through the dark rings his hurried stressed song, with the accent heavy on the first syllable. The singer is always afraid that someone may stop him before he finishes, and he hurries and hurries with a little click between the triads. At exactly eight o'clock, and again at just two in the morning, he sings there. Up in the mountains, where we once found the whippoorwill's two lustrous eggs lying like great spotted pearls on a naked bed of leaves, he sings at eight, at ten, and at three. Some people dislike the song. To me the wild lonely voice of the unseen singer pealing out in the dark has a strange fascination.

There are certain bird notes that strike strange chords whose vibrations are lost in a mist of dreams. I remember a little runaway boy, who stood in a clover field in a gray twilight and heard the clanging calls of wild geese shouting down from mid-sky. Frightened, he ran home a vast distance—at least the width of two fields. As he ran, there seemed to come back to him the memory of a forgotten dream, if it were a dream, in which he lay in another land, on a chill hillside. Overhead in the darkness passed a burst of triumphant music, and the strong singing of voices not of this earth. From that day the trumpet notes of the wild geese bring back through the fog of the drifting years that same dream to him who heard them first in that far-away, long-ago clover field. A few years ago there was a night of April storm. Until midnight the house creaked and rattled and clattered under a screaming gale. Then the wind died down, and a dense fog covered the streets of the little town. Suddenly overhead sounded the clang and clamor of a lost flock of geese that circled and quartered over the house back and forth through the mist. That night the dream came back so vividly that, even after the dreamer awoke, he seemed to feel the cold dew of that hillside and hear an echo of the singing voices.

It was only a few months ago that this same dreamer found himself on the shore of Delaware Bay, with the three friends who had gone adventuring with him for so many happy years. In the middle of a maze of woods and swamps shrouded in clouds of low-lying mist, they found at last the nest of the bald eagle for which they were searching. It was in the top of a towering sour-gum tree, and the great birds circled around, giving futile little cries that sounded like the squeaking of a slate pencil. As it was too misty to photograph the nest and the birds, the party started off exploring until the light became better.

Following the song of a fox sparrow, the dreamer became separated from the others in the mist, and after plashing through half-frozen morasses, found himself on the barren shore of the bay itself. As he stood there, with the white mist curling around him like smoke, from the sea came a clamor of voices. Nearer and nearer it swept, until a wild trumpeting sounded not thirty feet above his head. Around and around the clanging chorus swept, while, stare as he would, he could not spy even a feather of the flock so close above him. At the sound the years rolled back. Once again he was in the clover field in the gray twilight. Once again, on a far-away hillside, he heard that other chorus of his dreams. For a moment, in the lonely mist by the sea, he had a strange illusion that the life of which that cold hillside was a memory was the reality, and the present the dream.

It takes five years to understand Eskimo. It takes a long lifetime to learn bird language. At any time, in any place, the collector of bird notes may hear an unknown bird or a strange song from a known bird. Wherefore let no ornithologist vaunt himself. He may be able to distinguish between the song of the purple finch and the warbling vireo, or the chestnut-sided warbler, the redstart, and the yellow warbler, and then hear some common bird, like the Maryland yellow-throat, sing a song which he has never heard before and may never hear again; or an oven bird, or even a phœbe, rise to the ecstasy of a flight song which no more resembles their everyday measure than water resembles wine.

Early in my experience as a bird student, I learned to walk humbly. It happened on this wise. I had been invited to spend my summer at a Sanitarium for Deserted Husbands. Said retreat was maintained by a noble-hearted benefactor in a vast, rambling cool house, bordered on three sides by dense woods. The day of my arrival I was approached by one of the older inmates, who, with false and flattering tongue, praised my scanty knowledge of bird ways, and made me promise to teach him the different birdsongs as he heard them from the house.

Early the next morning, as I lay in bed, there sounded a strange song. It seemed to come from a tree at the other end of the house and possessed a peculiar rippling, gurgling timbre. A minute or so later my new acquaintance rushed in and seemed much pained that I did not know the singer. Thereafter my life was burdened by that song. Occasionally it sounded in the early morning, when I wanted to sleep but was awakened by my enthusiastic disciple. Another time I would hear it in the evening. One day it would come from the house, and again from the edge of the woods. Yet, skulk and peer and listen as I would, I could never locate the singer or identify the song.

The revelation came one Sunday morning, as two of us were breakfasting on the terrace close to the house. Suddenly that vile song began. It seemed to come from near the top of a tree by the farther end of the house. I rushed to the place, my napkin flapping as I ran. By the time I reached the tree, the song came from the opposite side of the house. Back I hastened, only to find that the bird had once more flitted to the other side. I hurried there, but again that bird was gone, and a moment later sang from the farthest end of the house. Three separate times I circled the place, with the singer and the song always just ahead of me. It was only when I noticed that my companion at breakfast had fallen forward on the table overcome by emotion, that I began to suspect the worse. I hid behind a tree and waited. A moment later I saw the alleged bird enthusiast, clothed in preposterous pink pajamas, and blowing false and fluting notes on a tin bird whistle, the silly kind that children fill with water and blow through. I have not yet been able to live down that birdsong.

When I was a boy, there were four of us who always hunted and fished and tramped and explored together. We never supposed that anything could separate us. Yet the years have blown us apart, and we go adventuring together no more. Alone of that quartette I am left to follow the trail that seemed in those days to have no ending. The same years, however, have made me some amends. Once again there are four of us who spend all our holidays in the open. We collect orchids and bird-songs, and find new birds and nests, and quest far among the wild folk in our search for secrets and adventures. Sometimes we go south, and become acquainted with blue-gray gnatcatchers and prothonotary warblers and summer tanagers and mockingbirds and blue grosbeaks, and other birds which we never see here. Sometimes we explore lonely islands hidden in a maze of sand bars, and discover where the terns and the laughing gulls nest; or we find wonderful things waiting for us on mountaintops or hidden among morasses and quaking bogs.

Two years ago we decided to follow Spring north. First we welcomed as usual the spring migrants and the spring flowers in April and May. When the sky pilgrims had passed on, and the lush growth of summer began to show, we traveled northwards to the top of Mount Pocono, the highest mountain of our state, and found Spring waiting for us there. The apple blossoms were just coming out and the woods were sweet with trailing arbutus. There we found the nests of the yellow-bellied and alder flycatchers, solitary vireos, and black-throated blue and Canada and Blackburnian warblers. As once more Summer followed hard on our heels, we took passage and traveled to a lonely camp in northern Canada. The second day of our trip we overtook Spring again, and were traveling through amethyst masses of rhodora and woods white with the shadblow. At last the apple orchards were not yet in flower, and for the third time that year we found ourselves among the cherry blossoms.

We never stopped until we reached a lonely bay far to the north. The sun was westering well down the sky when at last we crowded into a creaking buckboard for a ten-mile drive. The air was full of strange birdsongs. From the fields came a little song that began like a feeble song sparrow and ended in a buzz. It was the Savannah sparrow, which I had seen every year in migration, but had never before heard sing. At the first bend in the road we came to a bit of marshland so full of unknown bird notes that we stopped to explore. From the edge of the sphagnum bog came a loud explosive song—"Chip, chip, chippy, chippy, chippy, chippy!" The singer was a greenish-colored bird, light underneath, with a white line through the eye, and looked much like a red-eyed vireo except that it had a warbler beak, the which it opened to a surprising width as it sang. It was none other than the Tennessee warbler, so rare a bird in my part of the world that even to see one in migration was then an event. Here it was one of the commonest birds of that whole region.

Then I stalked a strange vireo song, something like the monotonous notes of the red-eyed vireo, but softer and with a different cadence. I finally found the singer in a little thicket, and studied it for some ten minutes not six feet away. For the first time in my life I had seen and heard the smallest and rarest of all the six vireos, the Philadelphia, so named because it is never by any chance found in Philadelphia. Its tininess and the pale yellow upper breast shading into white were noticeable field marks. To me it seemed a tame, dear, beautiful little bird.

Just at starlight we reached the camp, and I fell asleep to the weird notes of unknown water birds passing down the river through the darkness. Followed a week of unalloyed happiness. Each day, from before dawn until long after dark, we met strange birds and found new nests and listened to unknown birdsongs. One morning we heard a loud yap from a dead maple stub. On its side grew what seemed to be an orange-colored fungus. As we came nearer, it proved to be the head of a male Arctic three-toed woodpecker, who wears an orange patch on his forehead and shares with his undecorated spouse the pains and pleasures of incubation. As we came nearer, he flew out of the nest, showing his jet-black back and white throat, and fed unconcernedly up and down the tree, even when we climbed to where we could look down at the five ivory-white eggs he had been brooding.

Later on we were to learn how favored above all other ornithologists we had been, in that within one short week we had found such almost unknown nests as those of the Arctic three-toed woodpecker, the yellow palm, the bay-breasted, and the Tennessee warbler. We learned the jingling little song of the yellow palm warbler, who has a maroon-colored head, a yellow breast, and twitches his tail like a water thrush. Another new song was the "Swee, swee, swee" of the bay-breasted warbler, who wears a rich somber suit of black and bay. Over on the shore we heard the plaintive piping of the brownish-gray-and-white piping plover, who ran ahead of us and was hard to see against the sand. Right beside my foot I found one of the nests, a little hollow in the warm sand, lined with broken shells, containing four eggs, the color of wet sand all spotted with black and gray.

All through the woods we heard a strange wild, ringing song much like that of the Carolina wren. "Chick-a-ree, chick-a-ree, chick-a-ree, chick" it sounded. Then between the songs the bird sang another like a rippling laugh, and then for variety had a note which went "Chu, chu, chu" like a fish hawk. It was some time before we found that these three songs all came from the same bird, and it was much longer before we learned the singer's name. For days and days we searched the woods without a glimpse of him. We found at last that he was none other than the ruby-crowned kinglet, that tiny bird with a concealed patch of flame-colored feathers on the top of his head, who sings so brilliantly as he passes through the Eastern states in the spring. Not once during that week did we hear the intricate warble which is the kinglet's spring song. Evidently this talented performer has a different repertoire for his home engagement from that which he uses while on the road.

One of the most beautiful songs of that week I heard in the middle of a marsh, up to my knees in muck, water, and sphagnum moss. Around me grew

wild callas, with their single curved dead-white petals
and pussy-toes, grasses topped with what looked like
little dabs of warm brown fur. I was painstakingly
searching through the wet moss and tangled reeds for
the little hidden jewel caskets of the yellow-bellied
flycatcher, Lincoln finch, Wilson, Tennessee, and yellow
palm warblers. I had just found my fourth yellow palm
warbler's nest, all lined with feathers, and with its four
eggs like flecked pink pearls, the nest itself so cunningly
concealed in a mass of moss and marsh grass that the
discovery of each one seemed a miracle that would
never happen again.

Suddenly, out of a corner of my eye, I caught sight of
a tiny movement under the drooping boughs of a little
spruce half hidden in a tangle of moss. There crouched
a little brown rabbit, not even half-grown, but yet old
enough to have learned that maxim of the rabbit folk—
when in danger sit still! Not a muscle of his taut little
body quivered even when I touched him, save only his
soft brown nose. That was covered with mosquitoes,
and even to save his life Bunny could not keep from
wrinkling it. It was this tiny movement that had betrayed
him. I brushed away the mosquitoes and was watching
him hop away gratefully to another cover, when down
from mid-sky came a rippling whinnying note as if from
some far-away æolian harp. As I looked, a speck showed
against the blue, which grew larger and larger, and into
sight volplaned a Wilson snipe, the driven air whining
and beating against its wings in little waves of music,
and we had added to our collection of bird music the

famous wing song of the Wilson snipe, even rarer than the strange flight song of the woodcock.

A little later one of my friends found our first olive-backed thrush's nest, lined with porcupine hair and black rootlets, and containing blue eggs blotched with brown. Just beyond the nest I heard what I thought was a goldfinch singing "Per-chickery, per-chickery." The song was so loud that I stopped to investigate, and to my delight found that the singer was a pine grosbeak, all rose-red against a dark green spruce. All around us magnificent olive-sided flycatchers shouted from their treetops, "Hip! three cheers! Hip! three cheers!" and we heard the listless song of the beautiful Cape May warbler, with its yellow and black underparts and orange-brown eyepatch and black crown. "Zee, zee, zee, zip," it sang, something like the song of the blackpoll warbler, but lacking the high, glassy, crystalline notes of that white-cheeked bird.

I was responsible for the last birdsong which appears on the lists of my three friends—but not on mine. We were to start back for civilization the next morning, and I was walking along the riverbank in the late twilight, while my more industrious and scientific companions were writing up their notes and compiling lists of everything seen and heard on our trip. Through the windows of the gunroom I could see their learned backs as they bent over their compilations. Suddenly the eerie little wail of a screech owl floated up from the riverbank. Curiously enough, it came from the very tree behind which I was crouching. Instantly I saw three backs straighten and three heads peer excitedly out into the darkness. When I at last strolled in half an hour later, they told me excitedly that they had scored the first screech owl ever heard in that particular part of Canada. I never told them. It is not safe to trifle with the feelings of a scientific ornithologist. Undoubtedly my reticence in regard to that particular birdsong is all that has saved me from occupying a lonely grave in upper Canada.

Sweetest of all the singers, the thrush folk—what shall I say of them? of the veery, with its magic notes; of the hermit thrush whose song opens the portals of another world; of the dear wood thrush who sings at our door. While these three voices are left in the world, there are recurrent joys that nothing can take from us.

It was the veery song that I learned first. More years ago than I like to remember, I walked at sunrise by a thicket, listening to birdsongs and wondering whether there was any way by which I might come to learn the names of the singers. One song rippled out of that thicket that thrilled me with its strange unearthly harp chords. "Ta-wheela, ta-wheela, ta-wheela," it ran weirdly down the scale, and strangely enough, was at its best at a distance and in the dusk or the early moonlight. I was to learn later that the singer was the veery or Wilson thrush. That was many years ago, but I have loved the bird from that day. Once I found its nest set in the midst of a dark rhododendron swamp; and as the mother bird slipped like a tawny shadow from the wondrous blue eggs gleaming in the dusk, from nearby vibrated the whirling ringing notes of its mate. Again, on a tussock in Wolf Island Marsh I found another; and as both birds fluttered around me with the alarm note, "Pheu, pheu," the father bird whispered a strain of his song, and it was as if the wind had rippled the music from the waving marsh grasses.

In the dawn-dusk on the top of Mount Pocono I have listened to them singing in the rain, and their song was as dreamy sweet as the tinkling of the spring shower. The veery song is at its best by moonlight. I remember one late May twilight coming down to the round green circle of an old charcoal pit, by the side of a little lake set deep in the hills and fringed with the tender green of the opening leaves. That day I had climbed Kent Mountain, and seen my first eagle, and visited a rattlesnake den, and found a dozen or so nests, and walked many dusty miles. It was nearly dark as I slipped off my clothes and swam through the motionless water. The still air was sweet with little elusive waves of perfume from the blossoms of the wild grape. Over the edge of Pond Hill the golden rim of a full moon made the faint green tracery of the opening leaves all show in a mist of soft moonlight. As I reached the centre of the lake, from both shores a veery chorus began. The hermit thrush will not sing after eight, but the veery sings well into the dark, if only the moon will shine. That night, as from the hidden springs of the lake the heart blood of the hills pulsed against my tired body, the veery songs drifted across the water, all woven with moonshine and fragrance, until it seemed as if the moonlight and the perfume, the coolness and the song were all one.

Some April evening between cherry-blow and apple-blossom the wood thrush comes back. I first hear his organ notes from the beech tree at the foot of Violet Hill. Down from my house beside the white oak I make haste to meet him. In 1918, he came to me on May 3; in 1917 on April 27; and in 1916 on April 30. He seems always glad to see me, yet with certain reserves and withdrawings quite different from the robins, who chirp unrestrainedly at one's very feet. His well-fitting coat of wood-brown and soft white, dusked and dotted with black, accord with the natural dignity of the bird. It is quite impossible to be reserved in a red waistcoat. Some of my earliest and happiest bird memories are of this sweet singer.

The wood thrush has a habit of marking his nest with some patch or shred of white, perhaps so that when he comes back from his twilight song he may find it the more readily. Usually the mark is a bit of paper, or a scrap of cloth, on which the nest is set. Last winter I was walking across a frozen marsh where in late summer the blue blind gentian hides. The long tow-colored grass of the tussocks streamed out before a stinging wind which howled at me like a wolf. I crept through thickets to the center of a little wood, until I was safe from its fierce fingers among the close-set tree trunks. There I found the lastyear's nest of a wood thrush built on a bit of bleached newspaper. Pulling out the paper, I read on it in weather-faded letters, "Votes for Women!" There was no doubt in my mind that the head of that house was a thrushigist. That is probably the reason too why Father Thrush takes his turn on the eggs.

Once in the depths of a swamp in the Pocono Mountains I was hunting for the nests of the northern water thrush, which is a wood warbler and not a thrush at all. That temperamental bird always chooses peculiarly disagreeable morasses for his home. In the roots of an overturned tree by the side of the deepest and most stagnant pool that he can conveniently find, his nest is built, unlike his twin brother, the Louisiana water thrush, who chooses the bank of some lonely stream. On that day, while ploughing through mud and water and mosquitoes, I came upon a wood thrush's nest beautifully lined with dry green moss, with a scrap of snowy birch bark for its marker.

The song of the wood thrush is a strain of wood wind notes, few in number, but inexpressibly true, mellow, and assuaging. "Cool bars of melody—the liquid coolness of a deep spring," is how they sounded to Thoreau. "Air—o—e, air-o-u," with a rising inflection on the "e" and a falling cadence on the "u," is perhaps an accurate phrasing of the notes. Many of our singers give a more elaborate performance. The brown thrasher, that grand-opera singer who loves a treetop and an audience, has a more brilliant song. Yet there are few listeners who will prefer his florid, conscious style to the simple, appealing notes of the wood thrush. Although his is perhaps the most beautiful strain in our everyday chorus, to me the wood thrush does not rank with either the veery or the hermit. His song lacks the veery's magic and the ethereal quality of the hermit, and is marred by occasional grating bass notes.

My own favorite I have saved until the very last. There is an unmatchable melody in the song of the hermit thrush found in that of no other bird. The olive-backed thrush has a hurried unrestful song, a combination of the notes of the wood thrush and the veery. I have never heard that mountaintop singer, the Bicknell thrush, or him of the far North, the gray-cheeked, or the varied thrush of the West, but from the description of their songs I doubt if any of them possess the qualities of the hermit.

As I write, across the ice-bound months comes the memory of that spring twilight when I last heard the hermit thrush sing. I was leaning against the gnarled trunk of a great beech, between two buttressed roots. Overhead was a green mist of unfolding leaves, and the silver and gray light slowly faded between the bare white boles of the wood. A few creaking grackles rowed through the sky, and in the distance crows cawed on their way to some secret roost. Down through the air fell the alto sky call of the bluebirds, and robins flocking for the night whispered greetings to each other. Below me the brook was full of voices. It tinkled and gurgled, and around the bend at intervals sounded a murmur so human that at first I thought some other wanderer had discovered my refuge. It was only, however, the mysterious babble that always sounds at intervals when a brook sings to a human. It was as if the water were trying to speak the listener's language, and had learned the tones but not the words. Now and again the wind sounded in the valley below; then passed overhead with a vast hollow roar, so high that the spicebush thicket which hid me hardly swayed.

I leaned back against the vast thews and ridged muscles of the beech, one of the generations upon generations of men who pass like dreams under its vast branches. One of my play-time fancies in the woods is to hark back a hundred, two hundred, three hundred years, and try to picture what trees and animals and men I might have met there then. Another is to choose the tree on which my life-years are to depend. Give up the human probabilities of life, and live as long or as short as the tree of my choice. Of course it would be a lottery. The tree might die, or be cut down, the year after I had made my bargain; and I used to plan how I would secure and guard the bit of woodland where my life-tree lived. Of all those that I met, this particular beech with the centuries behind it and the centuries yet to come, was my special choice, for the beech is the slowest growing of all our trees. This one towered high overhead, while its roots plunged down deep into the living waters and its vast girth seemed as if nothing could shake it.

That evening, as I lay against it and bargained for a share of its years, I thought that I felt the vast trunk move as if its life reached out to mine. Life is given to the tree and to the mammal. Why may they not meet on some common plane? Someone someday, will learn the secret of that meeting place!

So I dreamed, when suddenly in the twilight beyond my thicket a song began. It started with a series of cool, clear, round notes, like those of the wood thrush but with a wilder timbre. In the world where that singer dwells, there is no fret and fever of life and strife of tongues. On and on the song flowed, cool and clear. Then the strain changed. Up and up with glorious sweeps the golden voice soared. It was as if the wood itself were speaking. There was in it youth and hope and spring and glories of dawns and sunsets and moonlight and the sound of the wind from far away. Again the world was young and unfallen, nor had the gates of Heaven closed. All the long-lost dreams of youth came true—while the hermit thrush sang.

Colophon

Angela Mazzara and Morgan Sacken, editing interns at Stockton University during spring 2017, edited this volume. Angela Mazzara completed final layout and text design during fall 2017. Tom Kinsella and Paul W. Schopp supervised the publication.

The text is set in 12-point Adobe Caslon Pro. The frontispiece is taken from the cover of the first edition. Gary Schenck designed the cover. Pagination does not follow the original edition.

The mission of the South Jersey Culture & History Center is to help foster awareness within local communities of the rich cultural and historical heritage of southern New Jersey, to promote the study of this heritage, especially among area students, and to produce publishable materials that provide lasting and deepened understanding of this heritage.